ENDORSEME

It is encouraging to see this subject addressed with clarity, biblical integrity, and accessibility. Stephen Beauchamp has faithfully served as a leader of the IHOP-KC prophetic, healing, and deliverance ministries, and now he has translated his many years of experience into a practical deliverance resource for all believers. I recommend this book for anyone interested in developing their understanding of spiritual warfare and strengthening their approach to pastoral ministry.

MIKE BICKLE
Founder, International House of Prayer
Kansas City, MO

Stephen Beauchamp has written a clear, practical book on very controversial subjects: spiritual warfare and the Christian ministry of deliverance. His treatment is evenly grounded in Scripture and personal experience. Rather than encumber the reader with thick, theological analysis, Mr. Beauchamp offers a simple ministerial approach to helping people regain spiritual health and wholeness. The book is a very good read.

CHUCK METTEER PhD
VP of Training/Academic Dean,
International House of Prayer University

Stephen Beauchamp sheds light on the often misunderstood topic of spiritual warfare. Through personal experience and Scriptural insight he will teach you to move in faith rather than fear to victory in Jesus.

EVANGELIST DANIEL KOLENDA
President of Christ for all Nations

Stephen is a good friend, a good man, and an effective minister. His book on deliverance is excellent. Rooted in Scripture and Stephen's own journey, its wisdom will steer you from common pitfalls and equip you with solid tools to help people experience Jesus Christ's delivering power. I highly recommend it.

ROBERT GLADSTONE PhD
Director of Kings People Church Charlotte, NC

My dear friend and comrade Stephen Beauchamp has done us a great service in the writing of *Power to Deliver*. He has taken out of the treasure chest of his ministry experience and godly character rich truths to strengthen the Body of Christ. Stephen's powerful anointing in deliverance is matched by his loving, pastoral heart. This book reflects both biblical truth and pastoral, practical insight."

ALLEN HOOD
Associate Director of IHOP-KC
President of International House of Prayer University

POWER TO DELIVER

POWER
TO
DELIVER

A Guide to
SPIRITUAL WARFARE *and* FREEDOM

STEPHEN BEAUCHAMP

DESTINY IMAGE® PUBLISHERS, INC.
P.O. Box 310, Shippensburg, PA 17257-0310
"Promoting Inspired Lives."

This book and all other Destiny Image and Destiny Image Fiction books are available at Christian bookstores and distributors worldwide.

Cover and interior design by Terry Clifton

For more information on foreign distributors, call 717-532-3040.
Reach us on the Internet: www.destinyimage.com.a

ISBN 13 TP: 978-0-7684-0716-7
ISBN 13 eBook: 978-0-7684-0717-4

For Worldwide Distribution, Printed in the U.S.A.
1 2 3 4 5 6 7 8 / 19 18 17 16 15

DEDICATION

I WOULD LIKE TO DEDICATE THIS BOOK TO MY WIFE SAGE BEAU-champ and my sister Cindy Graham. Both of these godly women contributed greatly to the formation of who I am today. The material in this book is the direct result of the sacrifice of their time and prayers. Thank you for every way you have laid your life down that I may know Jesus. You both have loved me well.

ACKNOWLEDGMENTS

I WOULD LIKE TO ACKNOWLEDGE JANE HARRIS TO WHOM I owe all the credit for the development and completion of this project. Without Jane Harris I could not have achieved this assignment from the Lord. Your reward will be great! And my family for all the ways they supported me in my calling and pursuit of God to make this book possible. The pastors, teachers, and leaders of the Brownsville Revival. My life has been forever changed from my experience during the time of the revival. The International House of Prayer in Kansas City for providing a place for me to grow in the knowledge of God through worship, intercession, and the meditation of His word. My dear friend Allen Hood who has been such a strength to me over the years. My King Jesus whom I long to see face to face—it's all for Your glory!

Thank you all.

CONTENTS

FOREWORD

SPIRITUAL WARFARE. DELIVERANCE. HOW MUCH DO YOU think about these important biblical subjects?

As I read Stephen's book, I was reminded of a time in my life and ministry when these topics received a lot more attention, and yet the spiritual realm hasn't changed at all and Satan's strategies are still the same. Why, then, do so many of us think so little about this very real and important realm of activity?

It remains true that our adversary, the devil, goes about like a roaring lion, looking for those he can devour (1 Peter 5:8). It remains true that our battle is not with flesh and blood but with spiritual powers in heavenly places (Ephesians 6:12). It remains true that all authority over Satan has been given to us in Jesus (Luke 10:19; Matthew 28:18). It remains true that the Son of God came into the world to set captives free, and we are His ambassadors, proclaiming freedom, deliverance, and reconciliation (Luke 4:18; Acts 10:38; 2 Corinthians 5:20).

Why, then, are the subjects of spiritual warfare and deliverance almost off limits in many of our circles today, including so-called "Spirit-filled" circles? If the Spirit is really moving in our midst, won't that bring with it a victorious conflict with the powers of darkness?

Perhaps we have been burned by unbiblical practices and teachings or by an overemphasis on Satan and demons or by various forms of spiritual extremism. Perhaps we have needed to refocus our eyes on the Lord Jesus and get our eyes off the enemy. To paraphrase a comment made to me years ago by a Scottish pastor, "The way some people talk you would think there was a great big devil and a little bitty God." May we never make such a grievous mistake!

The fact is, though, if we keep our eyes on Jesus and walk in the Spirit, we will come in contact with demonic powers, some of which are holding people captive. How will we respond? And as we seek God earnestly in prayer, we will have to engage in spiritual warfare. How can we pray effectively? Just look at how much Jesus and the apostles encountered demonic powers in the Gospels and Acts, and then ask yourself: Where have all the demons gone?

If they are still here (and they are), we need to know how to deal with them effectively and biblically.

In this very practical, faith-building book, Stephen Beauchamp, a spiritual son who graduated from the Brownsville Revival School of Ministry in Pensacola, lays out clear scriptural principles for deliverance, giving no place to the flesh and demonstrating real spiritual maturity. Based on years of hands-on ministry experience, Stephen has learned to avoid common pitfalls, to answer the most important questions, and to inspire real confidence in the Spirit's delivering power working through each of us.

As I read this book, I was convicted by my own neglect in these areas and I was stirred afresh to see the manifestation of Jesus' victory over Satan today as we war in the Spirit for the souls of this generation.

Forward!

DR. MICHAEL L. BROWN

CHAPTER ONE

THE POWER TO DELIVER

I GREW UP IN A SMALL GEORGIA TOWN, IN A CHRISTIAN HOME. My family believed in the present-day power of the Holy Spirit, and I was exposed to many of the charismatic gifts at a young age. I remember as a boy hearing my father stand up in the middle of church and begin speaking in tongues. I didn't understand what was going on, and more importantly, I didn't understand why the things I witnessed at church seemed to have so little effect at home. I probably could not have articulated this sentiment at the time, but in my heart I knew there was a breakdown between what my family believed and how we lived.

After years of painful conflict, my parents finally divorced when I was ten. Like so many others, I chose to respond by rebelling against everyone and everything—my mom and dad, my teachers, and even God. By the time I hit high school I was drinking and partying with older students, hanging out in clubs, and experiencing the drug scene. When I turned sixteen my dad bought me a car, and this created greater opportunities for me to immerse myself in the world of drugs. Soon I began driving into the projects of Atlanta to pick up crack cocaine. I had to tint my windows and call in advance before I showed up on a drug run in order to avoid potentially life-threatening situations.

Then things got worse. I was introduced to LSD and ecstasy at seventeen, and they became my drugs of choice. It was during this period in my life that I began to experience the realities of demonic activity. In retrospect, I can sort through my memories and differentiate between the hallucinations and demonic spirits, but at the time the lines between the two were fairly blurred. However, I do remember seeing creatures and dark shadows that I knew were distinct from the chemically-induced visions. There is a reason that taking LSD is referred to as "tripping." This drug's power to open up the human spirit and send individuals on a journey into the demonic realm was widely recognized during the 1960s and 1970s, when young people across the nation were searching for their spiritual identity through drugs and rock 'n' roll. My experience was no different; when I took hits of LSD, I often saw into the spirit realm, and sometimes demons would appear in the room and talk to me. Gradually my world was consumed by darkness, violence, and addiction.

One of the few remaining good things in my life was my sister. I moved in with her in my early teens, and she immediately began to wage war for my soul. She used to anoint my room with oil when I was out of the house, and pray over a handkerchief that she placed under my pillow. I was convinced I had her fooled—that my dangerous and illegal activities were a brilliantly kept secret—but in reality she knew exactly how bad things were. To this day it amazes me that she chose to let me remain in her house despite the risk to her family.

One morning my brother-in-law woke me up and told me he was taking me to get a drug test. My response was, "Why? I don't do drugs." He then proceeded to name my various dealers and contacts one by one. It turns out he and my sister had wire-tapped my phone and knew all about my secret life. When I realized this, I agreed to take the test and we drove to a nearby facility. I assumed it was a hospital, but once inside I realized I had been tricked. I was in rehab.

Although I was not allowed to contact anyone other than immediate family members, I managed to call one of my friends and ask for help in busting out. He later showed up with a ladder and hacksaw and tried to cut through the bars of my window! After that unsuccessful attempt, I gave up trying to escape and settled in to endure my time. It didn't take me long to realize there were a lot of patients in the facility with bigger problems than mine. Despite being a rebellious drug addict, I still believed in Jesus. I started reading my Bible, and even began preaching to some of the other patients. I remember sharing the love of God with a deeply troubled and suicidal girl; I actually led her to Christ despite the fact that I wasn't saved! God was clearly moving on my heart, but I wasn't ready to surrender my life to Him.

I was released from rehab after a few weeks—they could not compel me to stay unless they could prove I was mentally unstable—and I returned to my sister's house, clean and sober. For the first time in a long time I felt free. I truly believed I was a changed person, but in reality my journey into freedom (and the intense spiritual warfare it entailed) was just beginning. My system was free of drugs, but my heart and mind still belonged to darkness. Not long after my release, I met up with a group of friends at a high school football game and they offered me a joint of marijuana. I will never forget what happened next: as I began to smoke the joint, I literally felt demonic spirits enter my body. The experience was so dark, so intense, that I actually passed out. My friends attributed it to the strength of the marijuana, but I knew something far stronger was at work.

In Matthew 12 Jesus describes the danger of emptying our lives of darkness without filling ourselves with God.

> *Now when the unclean spirit goes out of a man, it passes through waterless places seeking rest, and does not find it. Then it says, "I will return to my house from which I came"; and when it comes, it finds it unoccupied, swept, and put in order. Then it goes and takes along with it seven other spirits more wicked than itself, and they go in and live there; and the last state of that man becomes worse than the first* (Matthew 12:43-45).

This was exactly what happened to me. I had grown up in the Church and so I knew about Jesus, but I did not actually know Him. And because I had yet to experience a true spiritual birth, there was nothing to fill the void left by the drugs, pain, and demonic bondage. Through the process of detoxification and counseling in rehab, I began to sweep my house and put it in order. But this was not enough. I needed more than a good cleaning; I needed to be made new. When I inhaled that marijuana at the game, it felt like everything I had gained during my time in recovery was sucked out of me in a moment. The bondage in my life really did increase sevenfold. I stood up after that experience filled with greater darkness than ever before.

For the next six months I engaged in the most severe drug abuse of my life. LSD, cocaine, crystal meth, ecstasy—I took whatever I could get my hands on. I started exchanging ecstasy for cocaine at a popular club in downtown Atlanta. The owner gave me VIP access, and my opportunities in the drug world began to rapidly expand. But my addiction was spiraling out of control.

> I needed more than a good cleaning;
> I needed to be made new.

That summer I went on a crystal meth drug binge. For two weeks I barely slept or ate. The binge culminated in a trip to Lollapalooza, a music festival known for its debauchery. I mixed LSD with ecstasy on that trip, which is a potentially lethal combination. The hallucinations I experienced were some of the most intense I had ever seen. I could feel demonic energy flowing through me and filling me. My friends were really concerned for me. They were afraid I was going to overdose and kill myself. But I was in way too deep to listen to them.

When I got back from the festival, a shipment of LSD I had been waiting for arrived in town. I took a friend with me to pick it up. Together we sold the majority, but I reserved some for myself. I knew I would have to double the dosage in order to feel anything with all of the other drugs in my system, so I took six hits. Soon after, my friend called with a warning. Apparently someone who purchased our LSD had taken half a hit and gone off the deep end. He stripped off all his clothes, beat up my friend's parents, and even broke a pair of handcuffs when the cops showed up to arrest him.

It is hard to describe how terrified I was when I heard this news. I had just taken six hits of this LSD—and it was so potent that just half a hit had driven a man crazy and filled him with supernatural strength. I knew I was in for the ride of my life. I told everyone to leave the house where I was staying, wrapped myself in a blanket, lay down on the couch, and braced myself. My heart was racing and I was scared out of my mind. I knew I had overdosed. I couldn't talk, couldn't move—everything was melting around me. The walls were moving and voices were speaking to me. I was convinced I was going to die.

In the midst of these hallucinations I heard a demonic spirit speak directly to me: "You are mine, and you are always going to be mine." In that moment something broke within me. I was filled with anger, and suppressed realities of the faith I had in God came rushing to the surface. I thought, "No, I am not!" Somehow I made it outside to my car and drove to my sister's house. My heart was still racing and I knew I was fighting for my life, physically and spiritually. I climbed into the shower and started singing a song I learned from my father. When I was little, he used to bring me to the church late at night and let me listen as he played and sang to the Lord. This is the song that came to me in the shower that night:

> *I love You, Lord*
> *And I lift my voice*
> *To worship You*
> *Oh, my soul rejoice*
> *Take joy, my King*
> *In what You hear*
> *Let it be a sweet,*
> *Sweet sound in Your ear.*[1]

As I was worshiping, the presence of the Holy Spirit filled the shower. I fell to my knees, weeping uncontrollably and thanking Jesus. I was so overwhelmed by the power of God I couldn't even feel the water falling on me. I didn't understand what was happening, I didn't have the language to explain everything I was feeling, but I knew God was there. I literally crawled out of that shower on my hands and knees and made my way to my room—the same room where my sister had been praying for God to encounter me year after year! As I knelt on the floor, trembling and weeping with my eyes tightly closed, I saw Jesus walking toward me. He put His arm around me and said, "I am faithful, and I will establish you and guard you from the evil one." He was quoting 2 Thessalonians 3:3, though I didn't know it at the time.

Immediately, in the midst of an overdose, I became sober. Despite my years of addiction, I had no withdrawal symptoms. I was set free in an instant. With just one touch, Jesus Christ saved my soul and delivered me from demonic bondage. From that moment, I threw myself into my faith as radically as I had once pursued drugs. I *knew* the power of God was real, and I was desperately hungry for more.

> "I am faithful, and I will establish you
> and guard you from the evil one."

I started attending services at a local church in Atlanta, and in many ways this was an incredible blessing. The members discipled me in my earliest days of faith (which couldn't have been easy), and they gave me a foundation in the Word of God. However, there were some inconsistencies in their approach to the power of the Holy Spirit, and this ended up creating trouble for me. I like to describe the church as an interesting fusion of Baptist and Pentecostal tendencies: they believed in the power of the Spirit, but there was enough structure and order to keep the more conservative members of the congregation happy. At the time, of course, I didn't understand the tension between these tendencies. I just knew that God was real and He had the power to heal, save, and deliver. I also knew the enemy was real and the battle for each and every human soul was inevitable.

I wanted to do everything I could to prepare for this battle. And so I walked into church looking for something real, something from heaven to fill me with light. I remember hearing messages preached on Matthew 10:7-8 and the power of God:

> *And as you go, preach, saying, 'The kingdom of heaven is at hand.' Heal the sick, raise the dead, cleanse the lepers, cast out demons. Freely you received, freely give.*

This was what I was desperately seeking! According to these verses, Jesus promised to release the power to destroy every work of darkness I had ever encountered. I eagerly anticipated seeing this power manifest in the lives of believers around me. Instead, I saw people who loved to talk about power but mostly lived without the reality. My anticipation turned to disappointment and frustration. Where was the healing and deliverance? Where were the things God promised in His Word?

> Most Christians hear hundreds of messages each year, yet have so little fruit to show for it. Have you ever stopped to ask why?

Many of you can probably relate to this disappointment and frustration. My experience is not an isolated one. Too many congregations are filled with leaders and believers who profess a theology of power but never see the manifestation. Most Christians hear hundreds of messages each year, yet have so little fruit to show for it. Have you ever stopped to ask why? Where is the breakdown? Why do we say we believe in God's power when we barely walk in it?

The answer to these questions is found in the book of James. Here, the apostle highlights a form of deception which has become widespread in the Body of Christ today:

> *But be doers of the word, and not hearers only, deceiving yourselves* (James 1:22 NKJV).

When we hear something and fail to put it into practice, we make ourselves vulnerable to deception. There are many ways this can happen. Some believers choose outright rebellion, refusing to obey God's Word, while others are held back by fear and brokenness. However, I want to specifically highlight a form of deception that I call "secondhand faith." It is not enough to know someone who knows someone who walks in the power of God, or to learn about the miraculous healings occurring in distant places. Simply hearing about the power of God secondhand is dangerous. The more we hear, the more we tend to appropriate these stories for ourselves until we can no longer distinguish between the testimony of another and the fruit in our own lives. We end up believing we walk in the power of God because we have heard about it. This is deception!

Art Katz, a well-known theologian and preacher, made this challenging statement regarding our tendency to divorce the Word of God from action: "Truth must be lived, or it will cease to be truth."[2] If we believe in the Word of God and claim to have received the authority to heal the sick, cleanse the lepers, raise the dead, and cast out demons, yet fail to exercise this authority, can we really say we walk in truth? You see, truth is not just correct information; truth is a Person. Jesus declared, "I am the way, and the truth, and the life" (John 14:6). The manifestation of truth ought to be the life of Christ overflowing from within the human spirit.

This reality characterized the ministry of the apostles. On the day of Pentecost, when Peter stood up and proclaimed the gospel, it says those who heard him were cut to the heart and three thousand were converted (see Acts 2:37, 41). The crowds were not swayed by Peter's oratory. Only weeks ago, they had cried out for the death of Jesus. It takes more than charismatic preaching to transform hardened, bloodthirsty men and women into repentant believers. This was the power of God anointing words of truth spoken by a radically surrendered vessel conformed to that very truth.

If Peter were to visit our congregations today, what would he say? We need to repent for seeking information rather than revelation, substituting doctrine for truth, and settling for a powerless form of Christianity. Please do not think for one minute that I am standing at a distance and condemning anyone. Every man and woman on earth operates in a certain measure of deception. This is why we are in desperate need of the proclamation of the gospel and the ministry of the Holy Spirit. When truth is anointed and illuminated by the Spirit, deception is exposed and we are empowered to choose life or death, truth or falsehood. Truth is never passive; it always provokes a response and produces change, whether positive (repentance) or negative (rebellion). There is no middle ground.

I am convinced the only antidote to the entrenched deception within the western church lies in acknowledging our lack and returning to the spirit of truth. I often tell my students that if I say I believe in healing but do not see anyone healed when I pray for them, then the only thing I should be preaching about is our desperate need for more of God. It doesn't matter how well I perform in the pulpit, or how many scriptures I have memorized. The question I have to ask is whether the people I encounter are being set free, because only truth has the power to release freedom (see John 8:32).

The absence of power in the Church was my greatest source of frustration as a new believer. Though I probably would not have used this language at the time, in my heart I was desperate for truth. I didn't want power to just be a good message. I wanted it to be a testimony, a reality in my life. This desire ultimately led me to Pensacola, Florida and the Brownsville Revival.

NOTES

1. Laurie Klein, "I Love You, Lord," House of Mercy Music, 1978.

2. Arthur Katz, *The Spirit of Truth* (Burning Bush Press, 2008), 4.

CHAPTER TWO

THERE MUST BE MORE

MY VISIT TO BROWNSVILLE

I remember vividly the first time I experienced the power of God following my dramatic salvation encounter. I had been attending church for a while, and had even joined the youth ministry as a leader. One Sunday, a youth pastor came to pray for us. He had just returned from visiting a church in Pensacola where revival was breaking out. In the summer of 1995, the Holy Spirit fell on the Brownsville Assembly of God congregation. Soon thousands of believers were arriving from around the world to experience what became known as the Brownsville Revival. I had never heard of it before, but when the youth pastor touched my shoulder and began to pray, I was overwhelmed by the presence of the Spirit. I instantly fell to the floor, and I didn't get up for two hours. I had no idea what had just happened, but all I could think was, "This is what I've been looking for!"

Immediately, I began planning a trip to Florida to visit this revival. Within a few weeks, I found myself standing outside a church in sweltering heat, waiting to get into a service. The crowds alone overwhelmed and provoked me. I did not understand why so many people were lined up in 105-degree weather, waiting for a church meeting to start. In fact, I did not understand how they even knew to show up in the first place! There was no advertising, yet people arrived by the thousands. This was a phenomenon to me. When the doors finally opened and I walked inside, I instantly felt the thick presence of the Lord. It was like walking into a steam room—I don't know how else to describe it. The atmosphere was filled with the glory of God. Psalm 19 says, "The fear of the Lord is clean, enduring forever" (Ps. 19:9). There truly was a manifestation of the spirit of the fear of the Lord in that place. It was the cleanest, purest thing I had ever felt.

As the crowd entered the building, some people fell down without anyone touching them or praying for them. I remember seeing a young man physically shaking and jerking as he walked—he looked like a chicken. I thought to myself, "That poor kid. He either has a disease or a demon. Something is clearly wrong, and he must be here to receive healing." I had never seen anything like this before, and in all honesty I thought it was weird.

Despite the unusual activity in the room, my curiosity was overwhelming. Suddenly, without any introduction, a man named Lindell Cooley walked onto the stage and began playing the keyboard. Immediately it felt as though the heavens opened over us. It didn't take any time for the crowd to enter into God's presence. No one told us to stand and prepare for worship. God was there, and we were all simply catching up to that reality. The experience was truly supernatural in its intensity. At one point I had to open my eyes because I thought I was being raptured!

After worship, a man named Steve Hill invited a group of teens to come up on stage and receive prayer. He invited everyone to stretch out their hands toward the platform and pray for the young people. As he walked up to each one of them, he began to yell the word *fire*, and one by one they dropped to the ground like wet noodles and started shaking uncontrollably. I knew they weren't faking it, because they were hitting the ground *hard*. I could literally feel the power and anointing emanating from the stage. I had never seen a man pray with such authority before. Steve declared, "The fire of God is here, and you can receive it. Raise your hands if you want to receive the fire of God."

I wasn't sure what to expect, but I knew I wanted more of God, so I closed my eyes and lifted my hands. No one touched me, no one began to pray for me, but I suddenly felt the presence of God dramatically increase and I dropped to the floor. Time seemed to stand still; though I was on the ground for several hours, it felt no longer than fifteen minutes. As I lay there, waves of the power of God rushed over me, like liquid fire rolling up and down my body. Charles Finney, the preacher and revivalist who spearheaded the Second Great Awakening, describes a similar experience in his autobiography:

> Without any expectation of it, without ever having the thought in my mind that there was any such thing for me, without any recollection that I had ever heard the thing mentioned by any person in the world, the Holy Spirit descended upon me in a manner that seemed to go through me, body and soul. I could feel the impression, like a wave of electricity, going through and through me. Indeed it seemed to come in waves and waves of

liquid love for I could not express it in any other way. It seemed like the very breath of God.... These waves came over me, and over me, and over me, one after the other, until I recollect I cried out, "I shall die if these waves continue to pass over me."[1]

Not only was I overwhelmed by the presence of God, but I began to shake and jerk like the young man I had observed earlier. And the shaking did not stop for three days. I had rented a hotel room with a friend, and the poor guy got absolutely no sleep! My convulsions shook the bed the entire night. When it was time to board our flight home, I was still shaking. I couldn't eat my peanuts or drink my soda! The other passengers probably thought I had some sort of disease. It was an intensely humiliating experience. I didn't understand what was happening, but I knew God had touched me. In Pensacola, Florida, I finally encountered believers who not only talked about power, but demonstrated it. The Holy Spirit testified to the truth of the message proclaimed by these men who had yielded their lives to Him and made room for the release of His power.

THE POWER OF THE KINGDOM

Many of us are guilty of compartmentalizing our faith. We might not confess it with our mouths, but in our hearts we believe the power of God just isn't for us. "There are some things every believer receives, like forgiveness, and then there are others that only the anointed few receive, like signs and wonders." This could not be further from the truth. Look at what the apostle Paul had to say about the kingdom of God:

For the kingdom of God does not consist in words but in power (1 Corinthians 4:20).

Power is part of the very essence of the kingdom. We cannot be simultaneously inside the kingdom and outside of its power. The moment we say yes to a life of faith in Christ, we are given the same Holy Spirit Jesus promised His disciples—the Spirit who endues with power (see Acts 1:8). This is meant to radically change the way we live, converting our reliance on our natural strength and understanding into a dependence upon and submission to something greater.

> Power is part of the very essence of the kingdom. We cannot be simultaneously inside the kingdom and outside of its power.

This is, in fact, the testimony of Paul's ministry. In his letter to the Corinthians, he reveals his complete dependence on the power of the Spirit.

And when I came to you, brethren, I did not come with superiority of speech or of wisdom, proclaiming to you the testimony of God (1 Corinthians 2:1).

"I did not come with superiority of speech"—but he could have. Paul was a Pharisee descended from Pharisees. He could have relied on his years of study, sharp mind, and powers of persuasion to convince the Corinthians of the gospel's truth. Instead he intentionally avoided these tactics.

For I determined to know nothing among you except Jesus Christ, and Him crucified (1 Corinthians 2:2).

This statement reveals an incredible level of humility and self-denial. Paul refused to use his own knowledge and charisma to draw people after him. The message communicated not just through his words, but through his life, was one of simple truth and power: "I know nothing but the truth that Christ died and rose again. The power of the Holy Spirit bears witness to His resurrection."

I was with you in weakness and in fear and in much trembling, and my message and my preaching were not in persuasive words of wisdom, but in demonstration of the Spirit and of power, so that your faith would not rest on the wisdom of men, but on the power of God (1 Corinthians 2:3-5).

Paul neglected his reputation and opened himself up to criticism in order that the Corinthians' faith would be rooted in nothing but Christ. How much of our faith today rests on the wisdom of men rather than the power of God? While Paul went out of his way to avoid promoting himself intellectually, today the Church is filled with leaders who advertise their own wisdom, rhetoric, and charisma. This has become normal throughout the Body of Christ; we are obsessed with how well ministers can articulate their message, and we respond to words rather than power. In contrast, Paul's ministry at Corinth was wholly dependent on the power of God to open eyes, move hearts and release the supernatural activity of the Spirit. Scholar Gordon Fee says it this way: "Paul knows nothing of a gospel that is not at the same time God's power, power manifested through the resurrection of Christ and now evidenced through the presence of the Spirit. That includes 'miracles' in the assembly (Gal. 3:5), to which Paul can appeal in a matter-of-fact way as proof that salvation in Christ is based on faith...."[2]

HINDRANCES TO THE RELEASE OF POWER

If this is meant to be the normal experience of kingdom life, why do we see so little reliance on the power of God in our churches? Why do we continue to compartmentalize our faith and justify the absence of power in our lives? I believe there are three fundamental hindrances to the release of power in a believer's life. These are not the only hindrances, but they are hindrances I have encountered personally and witnessed in the lives of many others.

The first has to do with our belief in the present-day working of the Spirit. There are many in the Body of Christ who believe the gifts of the Spirit (see 1 Cor. 12:8-10) are not available for believers today. This is known as cessationist theology, because those who subscribe to it think the power gifts have ceased to operate. There are many excellent resources which respond at length to the claims of cessationism and examine the biblical evidence for the present-day operation of the gifts of the Spirit. I will only address this theological stance briefly here.

In Acts 2, Peter stood up to defend the manifestation of the Holy Spirit at Pentecost:

> Men of Judea and all you who live in Jerusalem, let this be known to you and give heed to my words. For these men are not drunk, as you suppose, for it is only the third hour of the

day; but this is what was spoken of through the prophet Joel:

"And it shall be in the last days," God says, "that I will pour forth of My Spirit on all mankind; and your sons and your daughters shall prophesy, and your young men shall see visions, and your old men shall dream dreams; even on My bondslaves, both men and women, I will in those days pour forth of My Spirit and they shall prophesy. And I will grant wonders in the sky above and signs on the earth below, blood, and fire, and vapor of smoke. The sun will be turned into darkness and the moon into blood, before the great and glorious day of the Lord shall come (Acts 2:14-20).

Why did Peter make this claim? Joel said the Spirit would be poured out on *all flesh*, not 120 disciples. Joel also said there would be signs in the heavens and on earth, but no such phenomena occurred in Jerusalem that day. Despite this, Peter declared they were witnessing the fulfillment of Joel's prophecy. In other words, he interpreted the events of Pentecost as the inauguration of the "last days"—days marked by the outpouring of the Spirit and power. Human history now exists within the unfolding of this prophetic word. The Spirit has been poured out, and will continue to be poured out until the day of the Lord's return.

Peter ended by saying to the crowds, "Repent, and each of you be baptized in the name of Jesus Christ for the forgiveness of your sins; and you will receive the gift of the Holy Spirit. For the promise is for you and your children and for all who are far off, as many as the Lord our God will call to Himself" (Acts

2:38-39). He recognized the power of the Spirit was available even to those "far off" (you and me). If Peter said it, that is good enough for me!

It is also important to note there is no explicit statement in the New Testament declaring the supernatural activity of the Holy Spirit was a temporary occurrence limited to the apostles and the early church. Instead, we find numerous apostolic exhortations to walk in power, pursue the gifts of the Spirit, and expect the kingdom to break into our lives supernaturally.

Finally, the argument against cessationism I find most compelling has to do with the character and nature of God. When Jesus healed the sick, delivered the oppressed, and raised the dead, He was not only demonstrating His identity as the Son of God. He was revealing the heart of God.[3] The power was an expression of His nature. It said, "This is what God is like. He has compassion on His people, healing and delivering them." Again and again throughout the New Testament we are told Jesus came to show us the Father (see John 14:7-11; Heb. 1:1-3). If this is part of who the Father is, why would He suspend this revelation? Why would He give us His Spirit, but not authorize that Spirit to express His nature as Healer and Deliverer through manifestations of power?

> The power was an expression of His nature. It said, "This is what God is like. He has compassion on His people, healing and delivering them."

Based on these arguments and many others, I am entirely convinced the power of God is available to us today. However, I encourage you to search the Scriptures for yourself until you are satisfied with the answer you find. We cannot live on someone else's revelation. We must see and believe for ourselves.

The second hindrance to the release of power in our lives has to do with our understanding of the manifestation of the kingdom. When we study the New Testament, and particularly the Pauline epistles, we find two different descriptions of the kingdom's manifestation. On the one hand, it is described as a reality made fully available to us in the present through the power of salvation. When we confess Jesus Christ as our Lord, we are born into the kingdom of God. This is a literal transaction—our spirits are brought to life and transferred into another realm, and henceforward we are called to live in this new reality. We are given the power to resist and overcome sin (see Rom. 8:13); experience transformation in our mind, will, and emotions (see 1 Cor. 2:16); and walk in the realities of the next age—realities such as divine healing, supernatural provision, and victory over demonic spirits. Mark 16:17-18 says it this way: "These signs will accompany those who have believed: in My name they will cast out demons, they will speak with new tongues; they will pick up serpents, and if they drink any deadly poison, it will not hurt them; they will lay hands on the sick, and they will recover."

> Many theologians describe the New Testament perspective of the kingdom as an already/not yet perspective.

All this is possible because God the Holy Spirit is living within us. His presence, power, and nature reside in our spirit, creating a wellspring of life from which we can draw at any time. We are no longer bound to our old ways of living and being. In Matthew 10, Jesus exhorted the disciples to declare the presence of the kingdom of heaven wherever they preached: "And as you go, preach, saying, 'The kingdom of heaven is at hand.' Heal the sick, raise the dead, cleanse the lepers, cast out demons" (Matt. 10:7-8). As disciples today, we can make the same declaration: "The kingdom of heaven is available right now because I am a citizen of that realm. If you are hungry for more of God, then the Spirit who dwells within me will manifest His power in healing, salvation, and deliverance."

Based on these biblical truths, we can say we have *already* received the kingdom of God. However, there is another sense in which we are waiting for the kingdom. It is *not yet* fully manifested in our lives and in the earth. All we have to do is read the prophet Isaiah or the book of Revelation to recognize that the ultimate glory of God's government has yet to come. The Scriptures describe this kingdom as a place where there is no sickness, no sin, no pain, and no death (see Isa. 65:17-20; Rev. 21:3-5). Nature will experience perfect harmony (see Isa. 11:6-9, 65:25), wars will cease, and all nations will acknowledge the lordship of Jesus Christ. Clearly our present existence on earth does not conform to these descriptions, and it will not until Jesus returns and establishes His eternal rule on earth.

The kingdom is here and the kingdom is coming. How do we reconcile these two statements? The answer lies in wholeheartedly embracing both truths simultaneously. Many theologians describe the New Testament perspective of the kingdom as an already/not yet perspective. God's government has yet to fully manifest on the earth, but through the Holy Spirit we have been given the ability to receive and release the realities of the kingdom of heaven—realities which will be experienced in their fullness after the return of Jesus.

There are many verses that illustrate the present and future fulfillment of the kingdom. In his letters, Paul frequently describes the indwelling Holy Spirit as a present-day guarantee of future glory.

> *Now He who establishes us with you in Christ and anointed us is God, who also sealed us and gave us the Spirit in our hearts as a down payment* (2 Corinthians 1:21-22).

Here the Spirit is referred to as a pledge. A pledge of what? Of our inheritance—the fullness of the kingdom.

> *And not only this, but also we ourselves, having the first fruits of the Spirit, even we ourselves groan within ourselves, waiting eagerly for our adoption as sons, the redemption of our body* (Romans 8:23).

In Romans we are told the Spirit is the first fruits. We have been given power from on high, but this is just the first taste, just the beginning. There is a harvest yet to come, a day when we will experience face-to-face communion with the Father and receive resurrected, glorified physical bodies.

> *In Him, you also, after listening to the message of truth, the gospel of your salvation—having also believed, you were sealed in Him with the Holy Spirit of promise, who is given as a pledge of our inheritance, with a view to the redemption of God's own possession, to the praise of His glory* (Ephesians 1:13-14).

Again we see the promise of fullness inherent within the outpouring of the Holy Spirit. The power of God dwelling within our spirits is a pledge, a seal of promise pointing to the ultimate, eschatological day of redemption.

How is this understanding of the kingdom a potential hindrance to the experience of God's power? The answer is simple: many believers emphasize the future fulfillment of the kingdom at the expense of the present-day work of the Spirit. We become so fixated on the fact that the kingdom has not yet come, we forget we have already received it! It is critical we recognize the desire of God's heart to break in today, displaying His power in the midst of a lost and fallen world. This was how Jesus taught the disciples to pray. He told them to ask for the power of the kingdom, as it is fully expressed in heaven, to be released on earth: "Your kingdom come...on earth as it is in heaven" (Matt. 6:10).

In light of this truth, the question we need to ask is this: "Can I picture myself releasing the power of God and operating in the realities of the kingdom today?" Many of us need God to open our eyes once again to the reality that we belong to another kingdom, and we have been given access to the life and power of that kingdom in the present! Not only have we been given access, but we are exhorted to pursue the manifestations of the kingdom. Paul tells believers to "desire earnestly spiritual gifts" (1 Cor. 14:1). In the original Greek, the phrase *desire earnestly* can be translated *lust after* or *covet*. This is incredible; he is saying we shouldn't just talk about spiritual gifts or occasionally ask God to release His power. We should passionately run after the things of the Spirit and not give up until we see power operating in our lives.

If the belief that the supernatural is not available today is the first hindrance to living a "normal" Christian life of power, and an incorrect understanding of the manifestation of the kingdom is the second, then the third hindrance is outright resistance to the work of the Holy Spirit. I ran into this hindrance headlong after my first visit to the Brownsville Revival. When I returned home from that trip I shared my experiences with my sister and her family. They were incredibly receptive, and eager for me to minister to them. I remember praying for my nephew and watching him fall under the power of God, just as I did when Steve Hill prayed for the release of divine fire. I couldn't wait to see the Holy Spirit move in the same way at the church where I served. I didn't know it then, but I was in for a big disappointment.

> Many believers emphasize the future
> fulfillment of the kingdom at the expense
> of the present-day work of the Spirit.

After my experience in Pensacola, I continued to respond physically to the presence of God. It was as though my spiritual sensitivity had increased, and I was more vulnerable to the power of the Holy Spirit. I would frequently shake and fall down during regular worship services and ministry times at my church, and many found this behavior embarrassing and distracting. In addition, when I prayed for members of the youth group they began to experience the power of the Holy Spirit in similar ways. I was encouraged by this development and started praying for congregation members during altar calls on Sunday mornings. People began falling down under the power of God, but the general response was one of doubt. The leaders didn't want a twenty-year old kid running around and zealously praying for people, and they eventually stepped in and shut down my ministry activity. I was shocked. These people preached about the power of God and said they wanted to see the kingdom. So why were they rejecting the activity of the Holy Spirit?

> *But the natural man does not receive the things of the Spirit of God, for they are foolishness to him; nor can he know them, because they are spiritually discerned* (1 Corinthians 2:14 NKJV).

Although every believer has been given access to the life of the Spirit and the power of the kingdom, many of us are more connected to the physical and natural realities of the present than the spiritual and supernatural realities of eternity. We fall into the trap of evaluating life based on what we can see and understand, rather than relying on spiritual discernment. Paul states that when we are disconnected from the things of the Spirit, we find them foolish. This was my attitude when I walked into the Brownsville Revival for the first time. I thought the young man shaking and jerking under the influence of the Holy Spirit needed deliverance because I was convinced God would never do something like that.

Have you ever had the thought, "I'll believe it when I see it," or, "That can't be God," in response to hearing a miraculous testimony? These thoughts seem rational and reasonable to us—we even believe they guard us from hype and artificiality. However, if they are the product of our natural minds rather than the gift of discernment, then they are a manifestation of our resistance to the power of God. Such thoughts may actually be rooted in fear, pride, unbelief, and self-preservation. We all battle these strongholds to one degree or another. We are afraid of looking foolish, we are too proud to believe in things that defy our understanding, we are riddled with doubt and skepticism, and we resist placing our trust in anything we cannot control. Each of these mindsets hinders faith and shuts down the supernatural activity of the Holy Spirit in our lives.

This is one of the most common ways the enemy assaults believers. His goal is to prevent us from walking in the truth of all that can be accomplished as a result of the indwelling Holy Spirit. The reality of God's kingdom living within us threatens the strongholds of darkness, and so the enemy strategically undermines our faith and encourages us to embrace natural mindsets of fear and skepticism.

I remember a particular encounter that demonstrated the height of this warfare. I was out evangelizing, walking door-to-door, when suddenly I heard a young woman screaming. As I approached, she grew louder. She kept saying, "Stay away from me!" and it was evident she was involved with the occult. I finally got her to calm down and asked her what was wrong. She replied, "I was cursing you, but my curses weren't penetrating your aura." I explained that my "aura" was actually the Holy Spirit, and shared the gospel with her. She received Christ and was filled with the Spirit on the spot! When I asked about the curses she sent against me, she told me the primary way witches attack Christians is by cursing them with fear: "We discern believers in the spirit, and know the power they carry is greater than ours. But if we bind them with fear, they will never step out in faith and access the power available to them. They won't evangelize, they won't pray for the sick, and they won't walk in the spirit of truth." This is what the enemy is doing to the Body of Christ. He is filling us with fear because he doesn't want us to walk in supernatural power.

This makes me angry! Is it possible that witches and war-locks have a greater understanding of the spirit realm? Many denominations in the Body of Christ are still questioning whether supernatural power exists at all, while they are dis-cerning auras and cursing us with fear. We cannot treat our tendency to resist the power of God casually! At its core it is demonically inspired and designed to cut us off from our inher-itance. Remember, "the kingdom of God does not consist in words but in power" (1 Cor. 4:20). We must contend against fear in order to experience this truth—not just intellectually assent to it, but experience the manifestation.

This was Paul's prayer for believers in Colossi:

> *We have not ceased to pray for you and to ask that you may be filled with the knowledge of His will in all spiritual wisdom and understanding, so that you will walk in a manner worthy of the Lord, to please Him in all respects, bearing fruit in every good work and increasing in the knowl-edge of God* (Colossians 1:9-10).

We must contend against fear in order to experience this truth—not just intellectually assent to it, but experience the manifestation.

He did not ask God to fill them with natural wisdom. No, he contended in unceasing prayer that they would be filled with *spiritual* wisdom. Paul knew that the only way to please God in our walk is to receive the supernatural power and understanding of the Spirit. Without this we will not bear fruit—we will not see the kingdom manifest in our lives.

THE IMPORTANCE OF HUNGER

It is important to recognize our resistance does not always take the form of negative emotions (fear, doubt, etc.). Sometimes it takes the form of passivity. Many believers say they long for the power of God, but are waiting for Him to send revival. When the heavens are opened over their community, when angels appear and signs and wonders are performed in their midst, then they will step out in faith and begin to pursue spiritual gifts. Let me tell you, it does not work that way. I believe many people visited the Brownsville Revival and left without experiencing the power of God. It is sobering to realize our thoughts and feelings concerning the Holy Spirit may be the very thing preventing us from experiencing more of God here and now, and may hinder us from participating in the revival He will send to our nation.

Leonard Ravenhill once said, "The opportunity of a lifetime must be seized within the lifetime of the opportunity."[4] When a move of God occurs, we do not have the luxury of standing on the fringes, endlessly evaluating and critiquing. At some point our hunger must supersede our concern for the opinion of others. If we care more about what others think of us during a service than we do about what God might have for us, then it is time to seriously check our priorities.

The primary battlefield where we resist fear and contend for the things of the Spirit is the landscape of our mind and heart. It is an internal, invisible battle. However, in my own life this conflict played out externally in interactions with other believers. I was determined to hold on to the glory and power I had experienced in Pensacola, even in the face of pressure to "tone it down" and "stop being disruptive." I started taking monthly trips down to the Brownsville Revival to receive fresh encouragement. Eventually the Lord led me to enroll in the Brownsville Revival School of Ministry.

> At some point our hunger must supersede our concern for the opinion of others.

For the next two years I did not miss a single service, and I received prayer multiple times every night. Before I was saved, my appetite for drugs and darkness was insatiable, and I carried this same zeal and fearlessness over into my Christian walk. I did not care what I looked like, I did not care what others thought of me; I was going after God. There were many times I could barely walk out of the building at the end of the night. Sometimes I waited in the parking lot all night to save my place in line and be one of the first in for the next service. I had encountered the power of God radically when I received Christ, and I was determined to lay hold of it.

During my years of training at Brownsville, I was mentored by the head of their deliverance ministry. I remember many evenings spent in the balcony, surveying the crowds during the service while my leader pointed out the individuals suffering from demonic torment. Partly due to my own familiarity with the oppression of the enemy and dramatic deliverance experience, and partly due to my hunger for the power of God, I found myself profoundly drawn to deliverance ministry. This calling was confirmed during a three-month internship I attended in Paris, France, after I graduated from the Brownsville Revival School. Everything I thought I knew about the power of God and spiritual warfare was tested as I ministered on the streets of a city known for its practice of the occult. I learned experientially as I prayed for individuals struggling with witchcraft, homosexuality, and prostitution, among other things. I saw the deliverance of God, and I also saw the rage of the enemy.

I returned to the States in 2000 and then joined the International House of Prayer in Kansas City (IHOP-KC) three years later, where I have been on staff and operating in deliverance ministry ever since. The book you are holding in your hands is the result of over a decade of studying spiritual warfare and pursuing the power of God to save, heal, and deliver. You may be wondering why I place such an emphasis on spiritual warfare. Didn't Jesus tell us to seek the kingdom and let Him handle everything else? My answer is simple: you cannot walk in the power of the Holy Spirit without encountering spiritual warfare. There is an enemy, he is real, and he is waging an all-out war against the identity and purpose of believers. In order to see power released in our lives, we must awaken to the battle raging around us.

It is my desire to share with you the things the Lord has revealed to me along my journey. In the upcoming chapters we will examine the nature of power in the kingdom, the importance of knowing our enemy, and the process of deliverance. We will also look at the demonic systems established in the world to resist believers and the truths our enemy has sought to steal from us. I encourage you to talk to God as you read and weigh everything against the testimony of Scripture. Invite the Holy Spirit to be your teacher, and don't hesitate to ask the difficult questions! Hopefully those questions will begin to be answered as you go on your own journey in pursuit of God's power.

NOTES

1. Charles Finney, *Charles G. Finney: An Autobiography* (Westwood, NJ: Fleming H. Revell Company, 1908), 20-21.

2. Gordon D. Fee, *God's Empowering Presence: The Holy Spirit in the Letters of Paul*, (Peabody, MA: Hendrickson Publishers, 1994), 824.

3. "Dr. Michael Brown and Dr. Sam Waldron Debate: Have the New Testament Charismatic Gifts Ceased?" YouTube, 9:25 min., https://www.youtube.com/watch?v=CF0y5Csol_A, uploaded April 20, 2014 (accessed September 22, 2014).

4. Leonard Ravenhill, "Leonard Ravenhill's Ministry," https://www.leonard-ravenhill.com/quotes (accessed September 22, 2014).

CHAPTER THREE

WHAT IS POWER?

DEFINING POWER

And behold, I am sending forth the promise of My Father upon you; but you are to stay in the city until you are clothed with power from on high (Luke 24:49).

But you will receive power when the Holy Spirit has come upon you (Acts 1:8).

Have you ever stopped to consider how remarkable it is that after three years of teaching and training His followers, Jesus said they still weren't ready? He had answered their questions, modeled every form of ministry imaginable, and walked them through the Scriptures (see Luke 24:27), but it wasn't enough. The thing they needed was *power*. What comes to mind when you hear that word? Do you immediately think of God, or are your first thoughts related to worldly expressions of power—people who possess influence through politics, wealth, or celebrity? Perhaps you equate power with good preaching: "That was a powerful message." Or maybe you think it is limited to the regeneration of the human spirit at salvation.

> The source of God's power is found in the essence of His being. Power is not just what He does; it is who He is.

Sadly, few of us associate power with the Person of the Holy Spirit. This was certainly the case in my own life. In my early experiences with the supernatural, I learned to think of power primarily in terms of phenomena. Power was an "it"—something that happened which could not be explained by the laws of nature. After I was saved, however, I discovered that power is not an "it," but a "who." The source of God's power is found in the essence of His being. Power is not just what He does; it is who He is.

In the last chapter, we briefly discussed the ways our doubts and fears can limit the manifestation of the kingdom in our lives. This is a serious issue (and one we will spend more time exploring), but I believe there is another way we can limit the release of God's power. When we fail to cultivate a relationship with the Holy Spirit, we cut ourselves off from the true source of power and end up chasing ever-decreasing phenomena. Knowing the Holy Spirit, talking to Him, and meditating upon Him—these are the keys to releasing His presence and power in our lives. Have you ever stopped to ask yourself how well you know the Holy Spirit? So many believers fall into the trap of thinking of Him as a glorified Santa Claus who comes to distribute gifts. We relegate Him to this role and completely miss out on the relational intimacy available to us.

> ### Do we know Him and talk to Him as a Person?

Jesus placed great emphasis on the Person of the Holy Spirit. He actually told the disciples it was better for them that He leave so they might receive the Spirit:

> *But I tell you the truth, it is to your advantage that I go away...* (John 16:7).

Even in His resurrected body, Jesus can only be in one place at a time. His Spirit, however, can be everywhere. This is why Jesus said His departure is to our advantage. He wants all men and women to experience relationship with Him through the omnipresence of the Holy Spirit. And this benefit is just the tip of the iceberg.

> *...for if I do not go away, the Helper will not come to you; but if I go, I will send Him to you* (John 16:7).

Here Jesus refers to the Holy Spirit as the Helper. Other passages describe Him as our comforter, our teacher, and our guide (see John 14:6, 26, 16:13). These are all personality descriptions! And there is more—according to Scripture, the Holy Spirit has a mind, will, and emotions (see Rom. 8:27, 15:30; 1 Cor. 12:11). He speaks, He testifies, He prays, He can be grieved, He can be insulted, He can be resisted, and He can be quenched (see John 15:26; Acts 7:51, 13:2; Rom. 8:26; Eph. 4:30; 1 Thess. 5:19; Heb. 10:29). What does this mean? It means the Spirit is a Person with a personality. He is not a cloud or a funny feeling; He is the expression of God's inner nature. The question we have to ask ourselves is whether we treat Him accordingly. Do we know Him and talk to Him as a Person?

> *He will glorify Me, for He will take of Mine and*
> *will disclose it to you* (John 16:14).

Think about this for a moment: the Father determined it was not enough to send us His Son as a teacher, prophet, healer, redeemer, and savior. He did not stop there in His pursuit of our restoration. He had to take His own Spirit, the very depths of His personality, and give it to everyone who said yes. The most precious and sacred thing we possess as humans is our spirit. It is the core of our being, the essence of our existence, and we cannot give it to another. But the uncreated God is not bound by the laws governing human spirits. He can and does share His Spirit with us.

> **We are given full access to the deepest**
> **parts of God's being—His thoughts.**

This was the plan of the Trinity from the very beginning. Some believers mistakenly think that focusing on the Holy Spirit will rob the Father and the Son of their rightful glory. This could not be further from the truth. When we know and love the Spirit, and when we talk to Him and interact with Him as a Person with a personality, we are growing in the knowledge of God. The Holy Spirit lives to glorify the Father and Son by revealing their depths (see Matt. 10:20; Phil. 1:19; 1 Cor. 2:10-13). This is why Jesus said of the Spirit, "He will glorify Me, for He will take of Mine and will disclose it to you" (John 16:14).

Paul makes this same point in his letter to the Corinthians:

> *For the Spirit searches all things, even the depths of God. For who among men knows the thoughts of a man except the spirit of the man which is in him? Even so the thoughts of God no one knows except the Spirit of God. Now we have received, not the spirit of the world, but the Spirit who is from God, so that we may know the things freely given to us by God* (1 Corinthians 2:10-12).

We are given full access to the deepest parts of God's being—His thoughts. The things the Father and Son discuss—and the things they think and feel—all are available now through the Holy Spirit. As believers we are invited into the relationship and dialogue of the Trinity. It is time we make the Spirit our friend!

Not only are we invited into the conversation of heaven, but we are also given a supernatural power source for our sanctification. Holiness is as much a manifestation of God's power as healing and deliverance. The Holy Spirit enables us to live a life pleasing to God as He reveals truth and leads us into obedience. "And He, when He comes, will convict the world concerning sin and righteousness and judgment" (John 16:8). We do not have the ability to walk in righteousness on our own. The only way to put to death the works of the flesh is through submitting daily to the Spirit's leadership.

For those who are according to the flesh set their minds on the things of the flesh, but those who are according to the Spirit, the things of the Spirit. For the mind set on the flesh is death, but the mind set on the Spirit is life and peace, because the mind set on the flesh is hostile toward God; for it does not subject itself to the law of God, for it is not even able to do so, and those who are in the flesh cannot please God. However, you are not in the flesh but in the Spirit, if indeed the Spirit of God dwells in you (Romans 8:5-9).

*For if you are living according to the flesh, you must die; but **if by the Spirit you are putting to death the deeds of the body, you will live*** (Romans 8:13).

The primary way we submit to the Holy Spirit is through dialoguing with Him. This is so simple, yet so many believers fail to actually do it! Do we realize that the way we grow in holiness is by talking to the Spirit? When we engage in the conversation of the Father, Son, and Holy Spirit, we are growing in relational intimacy and uniting ourselves with the will of heaven. Jesus calls this "abiding."

Abide in Me, and I in you. As the branch cannot bear fruit of itself unless it abides in the vine, so neither can you unless you abide in Me. I am the vine, you are the branches; he who abides in Me and I in him, he bears much fruit, for apart from Me you can do nothing (John 15:4-5).

> Do we realize that the way we grow in
> holiness is by talking to the Spirit?

In this passage Jesus declares that when we cultivate a relationship with Him, we will bear fruit. How do we know this applies to our relationship with the Spirit as well? Because according to Paul, fruit is of the Spirit. "But the fruit of the Spirit is love, joy, peace, patience, kindness, goodness, faithfulness, gentleness, self-control.... If we live by the Spirit, let us also walk by the Spirit" (Gal. 5:22, 25). The more we grow in our fellowship with the Holy Spirit, the more we will bear His fruit in our lives and fulfill Jesus's command to abide.

MANIFESTATIONS OF THE SPIRIT

It is nearly impossible for me to talk about the power of the Holy Spirit without addressing the subject of manifestations. This is, in my opinion, one of the most misunderstood subjects in the Body of Christ. Let's ask the Holy Spirit to give us wisdom and discernment as we begin by looking at what Paul meant when he used the phrase "manifestation of the Spirit."

> *Now there are varieties of gifts, but the same Spirit. And there are varieties of ministries, and the same Lord. There are varieties of effects, but the same God who works all things in all persons. But **to each one is given the manifestation of the Spirit** for the common good* (1 Corinthians 12:4-7).

According to these verses, a manifestation is a display of power given to the Body by the Spirit to reveal God to the community. It is an empowering witness which enables us to more effectively testify concerning the truth of Christ and His resurrection. This is why Jesus told His disciples they needed to receive power before they could fulfill the commission to carry the gospel to the ends of the earth (see Acts 1:8). When we experience the manifestation of the Spirit, we are supernaturally equipped to do the works of God. This was the life Jesus modeled for us during His time on earth:

> *You know of Jesus of Nazareth, how God anointed Him with the Holy Spirit and with power, and how He went about doing good and healing all those who were oppressed by the devil, for God was with Him* (Acts 10:38).

In 1 Corinthians 12, after declaring the manifestation of the Spirit has been given to the Body for the common good, Paul goes on to list various gifts of the Spirit. The list includes words of wisdom and knowledge, faith, healing, and miracles. Some of these manifestations are physically discernible, while others are not. The common denominator, however, is the display of power impacting men and women physically, emotionally, and spiritually. Whether the secrets of the heart are revealed through a word of knowledge or the human body is restored through healing, supernatural power is testifying to God's presence and nature.

It is important to note the list of gifts found in this passage is not exhaustive. When we read through the New Testament, there are many accounts of the Holy Spirit releasing His power in unusual ways for the sake of the gospel and the edification of the Body. I want to take a moment to examine some of these accounts. Understanding how the Spirit operated in the early church will open our eyes to all that is available today.

The most well-known New Testament manifestation is probably the gift of tongues. In Acts 19:6, new believers began speaking in tongues when Paul prayed for them to receive the Holy Spirit. Paul personally experienced something even stranger during his own conversion. When Ananias prayed for him to receive his sight and be filled with the Holy Spirit, "there fell from his eyes something like scales" (Acts 9:18). We don't know exactly what these "scales" were, but this occurrence sets a precedent for the human body responding to the power of the Spirit in unusual, unexplainable ways.

Acts 5:5 documents another rare manifestation—death. A man and his wife lied to believers about a piece of property they sold, and both were struck dead instantly by the power of the Spirit. Can you even imagine what would happen if this occurred in a church today? You can bet everyone would be convinced it was the work of Satan and not God! In Acts 8:39 we see the manifestation of translation. Philip was supernaturally transported from one location to another—it says the eunuch he had just baptized "saw him no more."

Of all the New Testament manifestations, perhaps the one that stirs up the greatest controversy (in my experience) is the anointing of handkerchiefs and aprons. Look at the phenomenon recorded in Acts 19:

> *God was performing extraordinary miracles by the hands of Paul, so that handkerchiefs or aprons were even carried from his body to the sick, and the diseases left them and the evil spirits went out* (Acts 19:11-12).

The idea of God's power and presence resting on an inanimate object is offensive to our western minds, but this is consistent with the Hebraic worldview. The Jewish people would never conceive of a God who was not intimately involved with the physical world. This is why their systems of worship were so physical. Priests were literally anointed with oil, God's presence rested tangibly on the Ark of the Covenant, sins were transmitted to sacrificial offerings—the examples are endless. The manifestation of God's power on physical objects handled by Paul is simply an extension of this Hebraic way of thinking and being.

Hopefully at this point you are beginning to question your convictions about what God does and doesn't do. He is so much bigger than we realize and He is not afraid of acting in a way we don't understand or stirring up a little controversy. This is why we need to study the manifestations of the Spirit found in Scripture. We are so prone to putting God in a box— we memorize a list of gifts in 1 Corinthians and think we now know every way He could possibly show up. But this couldn't be further from the truth. Even as we adhere to the standard of corporate edification in our discernment of the Spirit's activity, we need to remain humble and open to the unexpected.

PHYSICAL RESPONSES TO THE POWER OF THE SPIRIT

In charismatic circles, it has become common to apply the word *manifestation* to physical reactions produced by the power of the Holy Spirit. This is misleading, in my opinion. As we previously discussed, a manifestation is a supernatural act of power that builds up and edifies the community. When someone is overcome by the presence of the Holy Spirit and falls down or begins shaking, the believers standing by them are not edified. Therefore, I believe such physical responses should not be called manifestations.

One of the negative effects of labeling physical reactions *manifestations* is the creation of inaccurate expectations. At the end of the day, physical responses to the presence of the Holy Spirit are personal. They are not an accurate measure of the Spirit's corporate activity. Yet we have validated meetings and movements based on these personal experiences. If people start falling down or shaking, we say it was a powerful meeting, and if they don't respond physically to the presence of God, we categorize the meeting as "less than." But this is not how God evaluates. The true measure of His activity in a meeting is the fruit of the Spirit growing in the life of the Body. We should not discount corporate gatherings or denominational movements because of the lack of physical responses to the power of God, nor should we expect to see these responses in every "powerful" meeting we attend.

Another negative effect of applying the word *manifestation* to personal reactions is the disqualification of believers who do not respond physically to the Holy Spirit. When we elevate personal responses to a "manifestation" or gift of the Spirit, people who do not experience them feel they are missing out or that God is withholding His good gifts from them. This can cause unnecessary emotional and spiritual damage in their lives and can undermine the unity of the Body.

In order to reverse these negative effects, we must return to the biblical balance of embracing the activity of the Spirit while differentiating between the personal and the corporate. Although we do not want to confuse physical responses to the power of God with the manifestation of the Spirit, we do need to acknowledge these responses as biblical and validate those who experience them. There are many examples in

Scripture and throughout Church history of individuals who were physically overwhelmed by the power of God. If we start to disdain the way the Holy Spirit personally ministers to men and women, we end up having to discredit the testimony of the Bible and nearly every major revival.

Many accounts of the First Great Awakening describe the heightened activity of the Holy Spirit and His effect on congregations. This revival is credited with galvanizing an apathetic church, spreading the message of salvation as a personal encounter, and birthing a new missions movement in the United States. Few would argue with the fruit of this move of God; it marked an entire generation and brought many into the kingdom. Listen to Jonathan Edwards's description of the "external effects" accompanying the revival in his region:

> The months of August and September were the most remarkable of any this year, for appearances of the conviction and conversion of sinners, and great revivings, quickenings, and comforts of professors, and for extraordinary external effects of these things. It was a very frequent thing, to see a house full of outcries, faintings, convulsions, and such like, both with distress, and also with admiration and joy. It was not the manner here, to hold meetings all night...but it was pretty often so, that there were some that were so affected, and their bodies so overcome, that they could not go home, but were obliged to stay all night where they were.[1]

This is not an isolated occurrence in Church history. During the Second Great Awakening which swept through the nation in the 1800s, dramatic physical reactions to the

Holy Spirit frequently accompanied the message of the gospel. Charles Finney, the great revivalist who preached to tens of thousands, recounts the story of his visit to a factory in his volume of collected sermons, *Experiencing the Presence of God*. As he was shown through the weaving room, a young woman working there began to exhibit signs of agitation. She laughed nervously, and her hands began to shake so that she was unable to mend the broken thread in front of her. Observing this, Finney walked toward her. Before he uttered a single word, she dropped to the ground and began weeping. Soon her companions had all joined her. This was the anointing resting on Finney's life![2]

The tangible effects of the Spirit were also in evidence at the camp meetings popularized during the Second Great Awakening:

> Similar behavior was associated with the frontier revivals of the Second Great Awakening during the early 1800s, where it was reported that...women would sometimes shudder so violently that their long hair would crack like a whip as they snapped their heads back and forth.[3]

Why did these women shake so violently? We don't know. We do know, however, that the revival they experienced brought thousands into the kingdom.

I want to briefly examine some of the most common physical reactions to the Holy Spirit. Why do we need to study these if they are not manifestations? The answer is simple: they are a part of many individuals' experience of God, and misunderstanding these physical phenomena can lead to confusion and division in the Body. Over the years I have found it helpful to evaluate the following physical reactions with these questions in mind: Do these experiences fall within the realm of possibility? Based on the activity of the Holy Spirit in the New Testament and in past revivals, is it possible that this is God?

Falling Out

There are many different ways men and women react to the presence of God. Falling out—also known as being slain in the Spirit—is probably one of the most common experiences within the charismatic community, and it has been documented in numerous revivals. Although there is no direct biblical precedent for it, we do find this interesting description in 2 Chronicles:

> ...then the house, the house of the Lord, was filled with a cloud, so that the priests could not stand to minister because of the cloud, for the glory of the Lord filled the house of God (2 Chronicles 5:13-14).

In Hebrew, the root word for glory is *kabad*, meaning "heavy" or "weighty." This suggests that the presence of God has a physical dimension of heaviness that can cause men and women to fall to the ground. At the end of the day, though we may not fully understand it, we can't argue that God is entirely capable of knocking people over.

In my experience, falling out can cause a lot of fear and anxiety. Many people are terrified of it and determine to only fall "if God knocks me down." This is the wrong heart posture! If we are determined to avoid anything that makes us feel out of control, we will not get very far in the kingdom. At the end of the day, resistance and fear distance us from God. He is the

One in control, and He knows how to address our individual needs. Let's be open to receive anything He may have for us.

Shaking or Jerking

We have already highlighted several historic accounts of this physical response (not to mention my own experience at the Brownsville Revival). Many people make the mistake of assuming that all shaking is a demonic manifestation. This is what I thought the first time I encountered it! We need to rely on holy discernment to differentiate between God's activity and the enemy's activity. Again, when we ask the question, "Is shaking biblical?" we need to consider that the human body has had far more violent reactions to the presence of God. If we can fall down or die in His presence, shaking is not outside the realm of possibility.

Holy Laughter

> And do not get drunk with wine, for that is dissipation, but be filled with the Spirit, speaking to one another in psalms and hymns and spiritual songs, singing and making melody with your heart to the Lord (Ephesians 5:18-19).

> For these men are not drunk, as you suppose, for it is only the third hour of the day; but this is what was spoken of through the prophet Joel: "And it shall be in the last days," God says, "that I will pour forth of My Spirit on all mankind" (Acts 2:15-17).

> For your love is better than wine (Song of Solomon 1:2).

Believe it or not, several times the Bible compares the experience of the Spirit to the experience of drinking. The imagery of wine reflects the Spirit's ability to soften our hearts and overwhelm us with joy. Based on the above scriptures, it seems safe to place holy laughter in the category of biblical responses to the power of the Spirit. Common experiences with the wine of the Spirit include falling, laughing, and speech impairment resembling drunkenness. While this behavior can appear foolish, it reminds us that God is not religious. He values the power of joy (see Prov. 17:22) and honors those who are willing to be made foolish for His sake (see 2 Sam. 6:12-22).

It is important to note, however, that this is not license for destructive behavior. We must always look for evidence of the fruit of the Spirit when evaluating a particular response. If spiritual "drunkenness" does not lead to an increase of love, joy, peace, and holiness, then we should question its origin.

THE NEED FOR DISCERNMENT

One last thing needs to be said regarding physical responses to the power of the Holy Spirit. There is a time and a place for the expression of personal encounter with God, but that time and place is not always a corporate meeting. I have been in services where shaking or laughter became disruptive and distracted those who wanted to hear the message. Paul addresses this issue in his letter to the Corinthians:

> *For you can all prophesy one by one, so that all may learn and all may be exhorted; and the spirits of prophets are subject to prophets; for God is not a God of confusion but of peace* (1 Corinthians 14:31-33).

In essence, Paul tells the enthusiastically charismatic church of Corinth that they are able to control their bodies, even when they are experiencing the power of God. This does not mean the physical reactions to the Spirit are not genuine! It simply means that for the sake of corporate edification, we sometimes need to curb these personal experiences. The Holy Spirit works in partnership with us—He does not overpower our will. When we respond to His presence physically, we are actually yielding our will and our bodies to Him. But at any point we can choose to stop.

Some people argue that shutting down physical reactions grieves the Spirit. If you look at Paul's instructions, though, you discover a different picture. The Holy Spirit loves the Body of Christ, and He wants to see Jesus glorified through the preaching of the Word. Therefore, if we control ourselves for the sake of those around us in a meeting, we are loving and serving our brothers and sisters and honoring the proclamation of the gospel. If you feel it is important to continue responding physically to the Lord as He ministers to you, you can always remove yourself from the corporate setting. Find a quiet side room or hallway where you will not distract others, and continue to receive from the Holy Spirit.

There is another category of physical reactions we have not addressed—demonic reactions. We will examine this category more closely in the chapter on deliverance, but it is important to say a word or two about the need for discernment here. It can be difficult to distinguish between holy and demonic physical effects. In both cases, the human body is reacting to a spiritual force, and those reactions can appear similar. The most valuable tools of discernment are fellowship with the Holy Spirit and experience. When we are in an environment where heightened spiritual activity is occurring, we cannot rely on our natural understanding. We must lean into the Holy Spirit, dialogue with Him, and ask for revelation and direction.

Over time, as we gain experience, our ability to discern between the holy and the unclean will increase. Usually there is an element of torment or aggression present in a demonically provoked physical response. However, we do not need to be intimidated by this. The Holy Spirit is in the business of shining light into the darkness. His presence may be the very thing exposing the demonic. When that is the case, we can rest assured that we are doing something right.

It is important to remember that skepticism and discernment are not the same thing. Often what we think is discernment is really fear-based suspicion. We need to remain humble, open to things beyond our understanding, and grounded in love if we are to truly walk in discernment. Yes, there are false physical reactions which need to be resisted. But the existence of the false points to the existence of the true and authentic. For every instance of hype, there is a genuine encounter with God. Do we want to miss out on the encounter due to our zeal for shutting down hype?

> Often what we think is discernment
> is really fear-based suspicion.

Many of us are contending for an increase of power in our lives. We want revival to touch our nation, we want more of God, we are even asking for signs and wonders to be released— yet when we see a few people shaking or falling down, we are instantly filled with doubt and accusation. "Why do they fall? Why do they shake? Why does God have to do it this way? Is it really God? Explain this to me. Is it demonic? Is it the flesh? That looks like the flesh. They are faking it. That is hype and manipulation." We have so little experience with power, we automatically reject it! Let's push past our discomfort and become students of the Holy Spirit. This posture of hunger and humility is the only way forward in the kingdom, and the foundation for discernment and spiritual wisdom.

NOTES

1. Jonathan Edwards, *The Works of Jonathan Edwards*, vol. I (Peabody, MA: Hendrickson Publishers, 2004), c.

2. Basil Miller, *Charles Finney*, (Minneapolis: Bethany House Publishers, 1942), 54.

3. *A Reader in Pentecostal Theology: Voices from the First Generation*, ed. Douglas Jacobsen (Bloomington, IN: Indiana University Press, 2006), 6.

CHAPTER FOUR

THE REALITY OF SPIRITUAL WARFARE

THE PARABLE OF THE SOWER

Up to this point we have examined the effects of unbelief, pride, and confusion in the life of a believer. We have discussed how these strongholds of the mind and heart hinder the release of God's power in our lives and prevent us from cultivating deep fellowship with the Holy Spirit. However, there is another barrier we will encounter as we pursue the power of God—the attack of the enemy. As I stated earlier, we cannot walk in the anointing of the Spirit without encountering spiritual warfare. Therefore, we must awaken to the battle raging around us.

My father was a faithful man of God and an anointed preacher who moved in the gifts of the Spirit. He lost his fight against cancer while I was attending the Brownsville Revival School of Ministry, but before he died he said to me, "If you can understand the parable of the sower and the seed, then you can understand all mysteries." This was the first parable Jesus taught the disciples at the beginning of His ministry. When they questioned Him about its meaning, He replied, "Do you not understand this parable? How will you understand all the parables?" (Mark 4:13). In other words, the teaching on the sower and the seed provides foundational understanding that unlocks the mysteries of the kingdom. And it is all about spiritual warfare.

> *Behold, the sower went out to sow; as he was sowing, some seed fell beside the road, and the birds came and ate it up* (Mark 4:3-4).

Jesus wanted to teach His disciples the dynamics of warfare. He wanted to prepare them to hold on to His words and produce kingdom fruit. Therefore, the first thing they needed to know was that they were in a war. "The sower sows the word. These are the ones who are beside the road where the word is sown; and when they hear, immediately Satan comes and takes away the word which has been sown in them" (Mark 4:14-15). Jesus did not pull any punches here; He wanted us to know who our enemy is and how he operates. As we listen to the Word of God, it is like receiving seed in the garden of our soul. But Satan waits to immediately steal that Word before it can take root.

This revelation is the foundation that will enable us to grow in wisdom and discernment, and produce a harvest of righteousness. The Body of Christ is in the midst of a crisis currently. We know we should be bearing fruit, but there is a lack of discernment. We must awaken to the resistance surrounding the preaching of the Word and develop an awareness of the enemy's tactics. We are in a war, and Satan wants to snatch the truth out of our lives before it can transform us.

We are in a war, and Satan wants
to snatch the truth out of our lives
before it can transform us.

It was common farming practice in first-century Israel to sow seed along beaten paths in the fields, and then to go back and plow the seed into the soil.[1] The fact that the seed fell beside the road is not necessarily the problem. Rather, it is the lack of follow-through and the absence of the labor of plowing that gives the birds opportunity to steal the seed and prevent a harvest.[2] This is a picture of the distractions, circumstances, and relationships the enemy will use to shift our focus and stop us from applying the Word of God in our life. These distractions don't just happen—they are the carefully planned tactics of an adversary who knows us well and traps us in cycles of unfruitfulness. Our own tendencies toward intellectualism and carelessness also contribute to the loss of the seed. Many of us delight in gathering information, but have no interest in the labor of applying that information. We fill our minds with messages, but the words we hear do not change the way we live.

> *Other seed fell on the rocky ground where it did not have much soil; and immediately it sprang up because it had no depth of soil. And after the sun had risen, it was scorched; and because it had no root, it withered away* (Mark 4:5-6).

This represents the second level of warfare. Jesus interpreted the seed sown in rocky soil as believers who delight to hear truth, but fall away when affliction and persecution arise (see Mark 4:16-17). This can take many forms—rejection from family and friends who disdain our faith, physical sickness, disappointed expectations, and even financial hardship. However it comes, suffering can be a devastating and all-consuming force in our lives. Have you ever gone through a season of financial crisis? All you can think about is where the next paycheck will come from, and whether you will be able to cover the bills. What about the pain of a broken relationship? Nothing eats at us like the fear of being alone or the loss of someone close. These things have stopped many from persevering in their faith. They may attend conferences and seminars and hear good teachings, but within a matter of days they are overwhelmed by the pressures and hardships of life and can't even remember what they heard.

Even those believers who persevere through ordinary trials can be taken out by persecution. Obedience to God heightens the degree of resistance we face in this life. We often experience greater persecution as we increase in the spirit of truth. Therefore the cost of our faith grows as we progress in maturity. Sadly, this causes many to stop running the race; some even fall away. Trials and persecution can cause us to give up on God, turn from Him in anger, or give in to the temptation to just survive. They expose what is lacking in our root system.

> *Other seed fell among the thorns, and the thorns came up and choked it, and it yielded no crop* (Mark 4:7).

> **We often experience greater persecution as we increase in the spirit of truth.**

The third level of warfare is found in the cares of this life and self-preservation. When Jesus interpreted the picture of the seed falling among thorns, He described believers "who have heard the word, but the worries of the world, and the deceitfulness of riches, and the desires for other things enter in and choke the word, and it becomes unfruitful" (Mark 4:18-19). We find a similar warning in the Sermon on the Mount. There Jesus rebuked the crowds for worrying about the things of this life—food, clothes, and all things necessary for their provision—and told them to make the kingdom their primary focus and aim. Only then would they experience the goodness of their heavenly Father and bear the fruit of righteousness (see Matt. 6:25-33).

This teaching point shows up more than once in Jesus's ministry because it is such a significant stumbling block! We are so prone to chase after the things of this world. Either we are consumed with materialism and the desire for comfort, or we are dominated by the fear of lack. These strongholds are reinforced through cultural systems set in place by the enemy of our souls. He knows just how to get us caught in cycles of greed and fear that prevent us from advancing the kingdom of God and bearing fruit.

> *Other seeds fell into the good soil, and as they grew up and increased, they yielded a crop and produced thirty, sixty, and a hundredfold* (Mark 4:8).

Most of us miss the supernatural promise contained in this verse. According to one scholar, "There is some evidence that a normal harvest was four to ten times what had been sown, and that a yield of fifteen times the seed sown was considered exceptionally good. On this understanding, the lowest producer of the good soil was twice as fruitful as anyone's highest expectations...."[3] This is what it looks like when the power of God touches our lives! The impact exceeds our greatest expectations as the kingdom is released and multiplied. Our ability to hear and willingness to labor will only take us so far. We need the ministry of the Holy Spirit to produce a harvest thirty, sixty, and a hundredfold.

I am convinced a great deal of pain and disappointment could be avoided if we truly learned the lesson of the parable of the sower and the seed. Spiritual warfare is not optional. It is a biblical reality experienced by every believer. And there is no middle ground. Either we will be overcome by the schemes of the enemy and stripped of our fruitfulness, or we will bear a harvest of supernatural abundance.

For to everyone who has, more shall be given, and he will have an abundance; but from the one who does not have, even what he does have shall be taken away (Matthew 25:29).

This is why Jesus took the issue of spiritual warfare so seriously—why He spoke about it in His very first parable and called it the key to understanding the mysteries of God. He understood it was a matter of life and death. We cannot afford to adopt a casual attitude when we know the enemy is coming at us with a three-pronged attack. We must equip ourselves with knowledge concerning this reality. The birds of the air are going to try to steal the deposit of the Word, persecution and tribulation will come, the cares of this life and the temptation of riches will come, but if we can hear the warning in this parable and learn to guard our hearts, we will walk in greater obedience and see victory manifest in our lives.

There is another important point that needs to be made regarding the sower and the seed. In the picture of the soul as a field awaiting cultivation, Jesus gives us one of the clearest insights into the growth and operation of strongholds. We will examine this subject in depth at a later point, but I cannot leave this parable now without providing a brief overview. The enemy is a counterfeiter, and in the same way the Word of God is sown in our souls like seed, so the enemy sows seeds of lies. Not only can we neglect and lose the holy seed, but we can actually cultivate and grow the unholy. Whatever we believe, think about, and act upon, we produce in the garden of our soul. As the seed is cultivated it first develops roots (these can also be called strongholds) and then a tree which produces fruit. Our lives will eventually display the landscape of our hearts— and if we are cultivating the seeds of the enemy, we will have a root system developed by lies and bear the fruit of bitterness, anger, sexual immorality, rejection, fear, etc. These are a far cry from the fruit of the Spirit Paul describes in Galatians!

> Whatever we believe, think about, and act upon, we produce in the garden of our soul.

KNOWING OUR ENEMY

Sun Tzu, a great military general who lived in China around 500 BC, wrote a famous book on strategy. *The Art of War* has influenced countless military leaders, and is still read and studied today. This is what Sun Tzu had to say about the importance of knowing your enemy:

If you know the enemy and know yourself, you need not fear the result of a hundred battles. If you know yourself but not the enemy, for every victory gained you will also suffer a defeat.[4]

This is no less true when it comes to spiritual warfare. When we are ignorant of the enemy's schemes or underestimate his strength, we fail to prepare ourselves for battle. There are areas in our lives that are vulnerable and in need of fortifying. Knowing who our enemy is and how he operates will help us strengthen what remains (see Rev. 3:2), avoid unnecessary losses, and walk in greater victory.

> Knowing who our enemy is and how he operates will help us strengthen what remains, avoid unnecessary losses, and walk in greater victory.

One of the most common misperceptions regarding Satan has to do with his power. We are so used to seeing images of a little red devil with horns and a pitch fork, and this media-driven characterization can carry over into our spiritual walk and alter the way we think about the enemy and the subject of warfare. How many of us have heard messages where the speaker confidently proclaims that Satan is under our feet? This is drawn from Romans 16:20, where Paul writes that "the God of peace will soon crush Satan under your feet." Notice he doesn't say Satan is already under our feet, or that we will do the crushing. Yet we sing songs with this refrain: "He's under my feet/He's under my feet/Satan is under my feet."[5]

Here is another example: How many of us have heard someone pray, "Satan, I bind you," or "Get behind me, Satan"? This language fuels the belief in a small, powerless enemy who will deflate in the face of a bold believer. Unfortunately, this is not the picture we find in the Scriptures. We are given clear promises regarding our authority over demonic beings (see Ps. 91:13; Luke 10:19), but nothing is said about our authority over Satan himself. While I do not want to glorify our adversary, I do suggest we check our assumptions against the testimony of the Bible and adjust our warfare tactics accordingly. As you read the following teaching points, ask the Holy Spirit to highlight any thoughts or ideas you have about Satan which don't line up with what the Bible says.

Have you ever stopped to consider that when Satan tempted Adam and Eve, they existed in a perfect state? They had glorified bodies, completely whole emotions, fully illuminated minds, and vibrant spirits. Their environment was without corruption—they lived in perfect harmony with God, nature, and each other. They didn't have family issues to work through, health problems, job fatigue, or "dry" spiritual seasons. Everything in their lives was covered by the glory of God. Yet Satan still had the ability to deceive them. At the height of created perfection, the serpent convinced Eve to question God's goodness and disobey His command. How was this possible? The author of Genesis writes, "Now the serpent was more crafty than any beast of the field which the Lord God had made" (Gen. 3:1). In other words, he was *smart*. He knew how to deceive the man and woman, he knew just how to target and exploit their weaknesses and manipulate the word of God.

This is the very first portrait of the enemy we are given in the Bible. He makes another memorable appearance in the book of Job.

Now there was a day when the sons of God came to present themselves before the Lord, and Satan also came among them. The Lord said to Satan, "From where do you come?" Then Satan answered the Lord and said, "From roaming about on the earth and walking around on it." The Lord said to Satan, "Have you considered My servant Job? For there is no one like him on the earth, a blameless and upright man, fearing God and turning away from evil." Then Satan answered the Lord, "Does Job fear God for nothing? ... You have blessed the work of his hands, and his possessions have increased in the land. But put forth Your hand now and touch all that he has; he will surely curse You to Your face." Then the Lord said to Satan, "Behold, all that he has is in your power, only do not put forth your hand on him" (Job 1:6-12).

This is unbelievable. Satan has access to God, and more than that, he can petition for the authority to attack believers. He even has the audacity to challenge the Lord face to face! When God speaks directly to Job in chapter 41, He gives a lengthy description of the "king over all the sons of pride" (Job 41:34). The entire chapter is a metaphoric portrait of demonic power, and throughout God relentlessly questions His listeners concerning their own strength: "Can you draw out Leviathan with a fishhook?" (Job 41:1). The point is driven home through the imagery—no man can catch a sea monster with a fishing rod. Look at the warning in Job 41:8:

Lay your hand on him; remember the battle; you will not do it again!

The Lord says if you try to fight this beast, you'll remember the battle and never do it again. It is a warning not to improperly confront Satan. Only God has the power and authority to master and defeat him.

Even the greatest Old Testament heroes of the faith knew what it was to be deceived and overpowered by the enemy. In 1 Chronicles 21:1 it says, "Then Satan stood up against Israel and moved David to number Israel." David, the man after God's own heart (see Acts 13:22), a mighty warrior and a passionate worshiper, king of God's chosen people and author of numerous psalms, was *moved* by Satan. He was persuaded to disobey God by the very enemy he swore to hate (see Ps. 139:21), and the cost to the people of Israel was dear—70,000 were killed in a plague.

Jesus was attacked by the enemy in the wilderness before the beginning of His public ministry. Satan was not intimidated by the Son of God. Three times he approached and tried to manipulate and coerce Jesus into sin and rebellion. Although he failed, he did not give up! Luke says that Satan "left Him until an opportune time" (Luke 4:13). In other words, he was not discouraged after losing round one, and eagerly awaited another opportunity to strike. In the gospel of John, Jesus refers to Satan as the prince of this world (John 12:31; 14:30; 16:11). He spoke of his defeat, but also acknowledged his current position of power and authority on earth.

Let's stop and consider Peter's experience with the enemy. This story is really crazy. In Matthew 16 Jesus asks His disciples, "But who do you say that I am?" (Matt. 16:15). Peter responds by confessing his belief in Jesus as the Christ, the Son of the living God. This is a divine revelation—Peter did not just come up with that answer on his own. Even Jesus declares the Father revealed it to him. Then He prophesies over Peter, stating that the revelation he received will be the foundation of the Church. (It is important to realize Jesus is not saying Peter will be the foundation of the Church. Rather, the revelation of Jesus's identity as the Son of God will be the primary building block of the Church.)

This is a high point for Peter. Known for getting things wrong, he finally gets something right! He receives divine insight from the Father concerning the Messiah, is given a new name with prophetic significance, and then is told the revelation he received will be the foundation of the Church. But look how quickly the enemy moves in:

> *From that time Jesus began to show His disciples that He must go to Jerusalem, and suffer many things from the elders and chief priests and scribes, and be killed, and be raised up on the third day. Peter took Him aside and began to rebuke Him, saying, "God forbid it, Lord! This shall never happen to You."* ***But He turned and said to Peter, "Get behind Me, Satan! You are a stumbling block to Me; for you are not setting your mind on God's interests, but man's"*** (Matthew 16:21-23).

Here was a man standing before Jesus Himself, filled with the spirit of prophetic revelation, and yet still vulnerable to the manipulation of the enemy! As soon as he started to think about preserving the life of his Lord, he opened himself up to Satan's influence. In a moment he went from prophetic revelation to demonic influence. This should be a sobering teaching point for us all. We are never too mature, too anointed, or too wise to fall.

Here are a few more New Testament warnings concerning the power of Satan. In his letter to the church of Thessalonica, Paul writes, "For we wanted to come to you—I, Paul, more than once—and yet Satan hindered us" (1 Thess. 2:18). The mature apostle Paul was prevented from entering a city by the enemy. We don't know the details of this confrontation; all we know is that Satan somehow stood against him and cut off his access to the believers in that place.

In his first epistle, Peter warns us to remain alert, for the enemy "prowls around like a roaring lion, seeking someone to devour" (1 Pet. 5:8). He then goes on to exhort believers to endure suffering and persecution with faith. All but one of the original twelve disciples were martyred. The early church knew firsthand how intense the resistance of the enemy was, and how costly spiritual warfare could be.

Even the angels have a healthy respect for their adversary. This interesting observation is found in Jude: "But Michael the archangel, when he disputed with the devil...did not dare pronounce against him a railing judgment, but said, 'The Lord rebuke you!'" (Jude 1:9). Michael, one of the great archangels, refuses to confront Satan using his own authority. Instead, he allows the Lord to be his authority and trusts in God for victory.

The important point to take away from these verses is that though our enemy has been defeated, he is not yet power-less. In fact, we have yet to see his greatest hour. Revelation 13 describes a coming day, just before the return of Jesus, when unprecedented power and authority over humanity will be given to Satan.

> *It was also given to him to make war with the saints and to overcome them, and authority over every tribe and people and tongue and nation*

*was given to him. All who dwell on the earth
will worship him, everyone whose name has not
been written from the foundation of the world in
the book of life of the Lamb who has been slain*
(Revelation 13:7-8).

Who gives him this authority? The answer is God. At the end of the age God will allow Satan to overcome believers and rule every nation through the Antichrist. Can you imagine the power it will take to carry out a global war against the Body of Christ and to deceive the entire earth? Even after the second coming, the battle is not over. Revelation tells us that at the end of the millennial reign of Christ, the enemy will be released from prison and deceive the nations one final time (see Rev. 20:7-10). People who have seen Jesus face to face and lived under His government for a thousand years will be persuaded to rebel against Him and follow Satan. Do we really know our enemy?

Satan's authority is not just a future reality; it is a present fact. In Revelation 2:13 we learn he has a throne—a throne of lies, a throne of murder, a throne of lust, greed, and pride. From this position he distributes assignments to principalities and demonic powers. He instigates murder, conflict, and war. He rolls out the homosexual agenda and gives license to immorality and perversion. He funds drug cartels and human trafficking rings. He issues decrees and floods the earth with false religion and deception. The evil we encounter in the earth is not haphazard. It flows from Satan's seat of power, and is distributed through a hierarchy within the realm of darkness.

However, this knowledge should not overwhelm us or cause us to lose hope. While we need a proper perspective when it comes to our enemy, we also need to remember how much greater our God is. In fact, the more we understand our enemy, the more we grasp the power and magnitude of Christ's victory.

> *For He rescued us from the domain of darkness, and transferred us to the kingdom of His beloved Son, in whom we have redemption, the forgiveness of sins. He is the image of the invisible God, the firstborn of all creation. For by Him all things were created, both in the heavens and on earth, visible and invisible, whether thrones or dominions or rulers or authorities—all things have been created through Him and for Him. He is before all things, and in Him all things hold together* (Colossians 1:13-17).

> *Therefore, since the children share in flesh and blood, He Himself likewise also partook of the same, that through death He might render powerless him who had the power of death, that is, the devil, and might free those who through fear of death were subject to slavery all their lives* (Hebrews 2:14-15).

THE FUNDAMENTALS OF DEMONOLOGY

We have spent some time examining what the Bible has to say about Satan. He is certainly our greatest adversary, but he does not act alone. The hierarchy of hell consists of numerous demonic beings. What do the Scriptures teach us about them? What can we learn about these enemies? The first point we should highlight is that demons are real. How do we know? Because they are presented as real in the Bible. Deliverance ministry was commonplace in the life of Jesus and the disciples as well as the New Testament church (more on this later). Based on this we can draw three conclusions:

1. Demons exist.

2. They interact with people in real, often tangible ways.

3. Believers are commissioned to walk in the authority of Jesus and cast demons out.

Let's take a step back and briefly discuss the origin of demons. There is some debate over this subject in the Church today. I have encountered at least three main theories regarding their nature and origin. Some theologians claim demons are the disembodied spirits of those who inhabited the pre-Adamic earth. This claim is linked to something known as the gap theory. In essence, the gap theory states there was life on earth before Adam and Eve were created. All such life experienced the process of evolution and then died off, creating a "gap" of time between the initial creation of Genesis 1:1 and the creation of Adam and Eve. Proponents of this theory believe the spirits of those who first lived on earth still roam today, seeking bodies to inhabit. This offers a possible answer to the question, "Why do demons want to possess a human body?" However, it does not line up with a literal interpretation of the Scriptures and the creation narrative.

A second common theory claims demons are the offspring of fallen angels and antediluvian women. Before the flood, Genesis records that the sons of God (angelic beings) procreated with the daughters of men (see Gen. 6:1-4). The beings produced by these unions were called Nephilim. However, there is not much scriptural evidence to support the theory that Nephilim are demons. Genesis clearly describes these Nephilim as "mighty men," suggesting they had the appearance and attributes of humans rather than spirits.

The third common theory regarding demons is that they are fallen angels. I believe the evidence of Scripture strongly supports this claim. In Matthew 12:24, Satan is called the prince of demons. This title implies that he possesses the same nature and characteristics as his followers, but operates in greater authority and power. Several times in the New Testament we encounter the phrase "the devil and his angels" (see Matt. 25:41; Rev. 12:7). The word *angel* is applied to the demonic entities under the command of Satan, again suggesting that demons are fallen angels. Finally, we see the same metaphoric language used to characterize Satan and his followers. In two different passages Satan is described as a star fallen to earth (see Isa. 14:12; Luke 10:18). Similarly, when the book of Revelation describes his initial rebellion, it says he swept a third of the stars out of heaven (see Rev. 12:4). Using Scripture to interpret Scripture, this suggests a third of the angels followed Satan and were cast out of heaven.

If we accept that demons are fallen angels, there is an important point we need to be clear about. Although God created the angels, including Lucifer (another name for Satan found in Isaiah 14:12), God did not create evil. The mystery of free will and the sovereignty of God is one we will never fully comprehend on this side of eternity. All we can do is wrestle with the knowledge that He foresaw creation would rebel and choose evil, and in His goodness and sovereignty He allowed it. In the process of this wrestling, our hearts are tested, mature love is produced within us, and we grow in dependency on God.

Now I want to briefly examine what the Bible has to say about the nature of demons. In both Hebrew and Greek, the word for "spirit" carries the meaning of breath or wind. While there is a certain element of mystery concerning the nature of spiritual beings, the Bible presents this analogy to help us comprehend what we cannot see. Demons are not flesh-and-blood creatures. They are of the spirit, and therefore able to inhabit physical vessels in the way breath fills the human body. The gospels tell us of one instance where a legion of demons left a man and entered into a herd of swine (see Mark 5:12-13). It does not say the demons were visible to the human eye when they exited the man. Like the wind, their presence remained invisible. However, the effect they had on their hosts was immediate and dramatic evidence of their activity—the entire herd of swine rushed off the edge of a cliff and drowned in the sea.

Because demons are spirits, when they are cast out we sometimes see an accompanying manifestation of wind released, such as coughing, burping, sneezing, or gas. Occasionally a person may even vomit when a spirit is leaving them. However, none of these reactions are necessary to the deliverance process. We will address this subject later in greater depth.

Though demons are spiritual beings, they can take on physical form. In the book of Daniel we learn an angel with the appearance of a man was locked in combat with a demonic principality (the prince of the kingdom of Persia) for twenty-one days (see Dan. 10:12-16). Based on this, we can infer the demon also had the appearance of a man. In the book of Revelation, we find several descriptions of demonic beings in the form of unusual creatures, such as locusts and frogs (see Rev. 9:7-11; 16:13-14). Heaven is inhabited by angels with many different forms, some of which we would describe as creatures. (See Ezekiel's description of the living creatures in Ezekiel 1:5-14, or John's description in Revelation 4:6-8.) I believe that when Satan fell, some of these creatures followed him as part of the company of rebelling angelic spirits. This would explain why people often report seeing unusual, gargoyle-like beings when they encounter demons. However, it is not necessarily important that we understand why spirits possess different forms, or why they may seek to inhabit human bodies. It is enough to know this is the case, and rest in the authority we have been given in Christ to cast them out.

In addition to addressing their nature as spiritual beings, the Scriptures describe the great strength of demons. In the Gospel of Mark, Jesus encountered a man possessed by an unclean spirit:

> *When He got out of the boat, immediately a man from the tombs with an unclean spirit met Him, and he had his dwelling among the tombs. And no one was able to bind him anymore, even with a chain; because he had often been bound with shackles and chains, and the chains had been torn apart by him and the shackles broken in pieces, and no one was strong enough to subdue him* (Mark 5:2-4).

The demon in this man produced superhuman strength. He was able to break through chains, and no one was strong enough to physically constrain him. There is a similar account found in the book of Acts. A man possessed by an evil spirit overpowered seven men, and they fled from him wounded and naked (see Acts 19:14-16). I have seen such manifestations for myself—remember the guy who overdosed on the LSD I sold him, beat up my friend's parents, and broke a pair of handcuffs when the cops tried to arrest him? He was clearly under the influence of more than just drugs.

Another thing we learn from the testimony of Scripture is that demons are not omniscient. We see instances where demons recognize Jesus (see Mark 1:34; Luke 4:41), we see them acknowledge their ultimate fate (see Matt. 8:29), and we even see them recognize individual believers by reputation (see Acts 19:15)—but we never see evidence suggesting they are all-knowing.

Finally, the Scriptures describe demons as evil, unclean, and lying spirits (see Luke 11:24-26). When talking about Satan, Jesus calls him the father of lies and declares there is no truth in his nature:

> *He was a murderer from the beginning, and does not stand in the truth because there is no truth in him. Whenever he speaks a lie, he speaks from his own nature, for he is a liar and the father of lies* (John 8:44).

This description applies not only to the enemy, but also to his followers. Demons have no truth in them; they only speak lies, distortions, and perversions. It is their identity and their mode of operation. Remembering this will help us combat their influence in our lives.

When we look at the world around us, it is not hard to see evidence of demonic influence. In fact, I believe we are currently seeing the escalation of wickedness across the earth. Now more than ever we must awaken to the reality of the enemy we face, fight for freedom in our own lives, and equip ourselves to set the captives free.

In the next chapters I want to examine the ministry of deliverance. This ministry is the frontline in the spiritual battle for humanity. However, it has developed a negative reputation in much of the Body of Christ. Deliverance is viewed as an elite calling reserved for the highly discerning and anointed, or worse, as a breeding ground for every weird and wacky spiritual practice. Over the years I have read various books on this subject and experienced many different ministry models—and I want to help you avoid the mistakes I've made! I want to see the stigma of deliverance broken and a biblical understanding established in its place. All believers are called to pray for others and see them set free. This is our holy and precious inheritance in the Lord.

NOTES

1. M. Eugene Boring, *Mark: A Commentary* (Louisville, KY: Westminster John Knox Press, 2006), 117.

2. Ibid.

3. Ibid., 118.

4. Sun Tzu, *The Art of War*, translated by Lionel Giles, special ed. (El Paso, TX: El Paso Norte Press, 2005), 132.

5. Richard Black, *Enemy's Camp*, Sound III, Inc., 1991.

CHAPTER FIVE

EXPOSING THE SCHEMES OF THE ENEMY

THE FUNDAMENTALS OF STRONGHOLDS: ACCESS POINTS

We have looked at the nature of demons (who they are); now we will examine the nature of strongholds (how demons operate in our lives). It is important to understand the way strongholds are formed before we begin pursuing deliverance. Without this understanding, we will remain vulnerable to deception and bondage.

When God formed humanity in the garden, He created us with a three-part nature. Paul references this fact in his letter to the Thessalonians:

> *Now may the God of peace Himself sanctify you entirely;* **and may your spirit and soul and body be preserved complete**, *without blame at*

the coming of our Lord Jesus Christ (1 Thessa-lonians 5:23).

These three components together form the entirety of a person. The body is a physical shell which houses the soul and the spirit. The soul consists of our mind, will, and emotions. This is where we think, make decisions, experience emotions, and display our unique identity as a person. The spirit is where we commune with God. According to the testimony of Scripture, God created men and women in His image and likeness, with living spirits, so we might relate to Him (see Gen. 1:26; 2:7; John 4:24).

When demons form strongholds in our lives, they target the soul. However, before they can build strongholds they need an access point—a way into the soul. Most access points can be divided into four general categories.

1. Trauma

2. The five senses

3. Deception

4. Generational sins

This is not an exhaustive list, and these categories are not rigid. In fact, there is a great deal of overlap between the four categories—we experience trauma physically (with our senses), deception is often passed down through generational sins, and generational sins can produce trauma. This list is simply a tool intended to help us identify places of vulnerability in our own lives and the lives of those we are walking through deliverance. The most important thing to notice is that all four categories involve sin, whether voluntary or involuntary. At the end of the day, sin is the only thing which gives an unclean spirit the right to enter our lives.

Trauma

It is incredibly common for people who have experienced trauma to be vulnerable to the attack of the enemy. Trauma can include any form of tragedy or loss, such as the death of a loved one; abuse of any kind, whether physical, verbal, sexual, emotional, or spiritual; accidents and near death experiences; or any intense occurrence which produces fear. When these things touch a person's life, they can be exposed to heightened levels of darkness which barrage their psyche and cause them to accept the lies accompanying that darkness. In fact, some of the greatest demonic strongholds are built on the foundation of trauma. When demonic activity is affecting a person's mental health or manifesting through them physically to the point where they exhibit supernatural strength or speak in different voices, there is usually a history of trauma in their life. The violent nature of the enemy's access point in their life enables him to take ground quickly, and the individual may end up psychologically dominated.

The Five Senses

There are many ways demons can gain access to us through our senses. The five senses have often been called the gates to the soul, and I believe this is an accurate metaphor. When we participate in sin through the things we see and hear or through our words and actions, we are allowing that sin to enter our soul. Let me be very clear on this point—we do not need deliverance if we accidentally view a sex scene in a movie or listen to a secular song playing in a store. Simply being exposed to darkness does not demonize us. The enemy only has legal access to our souls when we *agree with* and *participate in* the darkness in front of us. We have the ability to draw a line within our own souls and declare, "I do not agree with this!" when that scene shows up on the screen or that song starts playing on the radio. In this way, we refuse entrance to the demonic spirit fueling the darkness.

> The five senses have often been called
> the gates to the soul, and I believe
> this is an accurate metaphor.

There is a very real need for caution when it comes to the issue of entertainment and media. As human beings we are created for connection. We are designed to be sensitive to others emotionally and spiritually. We have the ability to empathize—to literally "feel with" them. When this sensitivity causes us to identify with the brokenness of unbelievers, we open ourselves to the demonic spirits operating in their lives. I remember hearing the Smashing Pumpkins and the Beastie Boys perform at Lollapalooza before I was saved. As these bands played, my hallucinations and demonic encounters dramatically increased. In particular, I recall feeling demonic energy being imparted to me as I participated in a mosh pit while the Beastie Boys performed. Just as the Holy Spirit anoints worshipers to escort believers into heavenly encounters, the enemy anoints secular bands to draw people into demonic encounters through their songs. This is why believers need to walk in discernment when it comes to entertainment and media.

Many people feel that any warning related to music and movies is legalistic. While we want to avoid legalism and leave room for every believer to individually seek the Holy Spirit for discernment, we also need to acknowledge the war around us.

Secular artists and entertainers often confront our theology and ask us to participate in their worldview. The more we do so willingly, the more we open ourselves to the enemy. At the same time we need to remember how kind God is when dealing with our immaturity. He is desperate to speak to us, and if we are not filling ourselves with His Word, He will use any available means of communication. This is usually what is happening when someone feels God speaking to them through a favorite movie or song. Right after my salvation encounter, God spoke to me powerfully through a TV show I was watching. However, I believe His highest will for our lives is that we would encounter Him in His Word and during times of direct communion. Hearing God through secular media is the lowest form of revelation.

> Hearing God through secular media
> is the lowest form of revelation.

Although I have emphasized our eyes and ears in the discussion of the senses, it is important to note we can also open ourselves to the enemy through sinful physical behaviors and the words we speak. Drugs, alcohol, and sexual immorality are all open doors in our lives. The things we say about ourselves and others can be just as damaging, making us vulnerable to self-hatred, judgment, and unrighteous relational conflict.

Deception

Deception is the third common access point utilized by the enemy. Many of us associate deception with extreme cults, but the truth is we all have deception operating at some level in our lives. It frequently comes in the form of lies we believe about our identity and worth and accusations in our hearts against others. Of course, deception is also at work in any type of doctrinal error or false teaching, as well as every occult practice and false religion. There is no place for magic, new-age spirituality, or the beliefs of other religions in our lives!

Generational Sins

The fourth general access point for the demonic in our lives comes from generational sins and demonic assignments. We inherit more than physical traits from our parents. Addictions, patterns of behavior, and character weaknesses are also passed down through family lines. Often the struggles we label "personality traits," such as laziness or a short temper, are actually the product of demonic strongholds normalized within our childhood homes. We need the Holy Spirit to illuminate the areas of our life where He is not in control, and commit to tear down even the most familiar and comfortable patterns of thinking and living that resist His leadership.

It is important to distinguish between demonic generational assignments and Deuteronomic curses. According to the Law of Moses, God promises to visit the iniquity of the fathers on the children down to the third and fourth generations (see Deut. 5:9). This law still stands for unbelievers, but if you are a believer you are no longer under the law. God is not holding you accountable for the sins of your parents and grandparents. Jesus became a curse for you when He hung on the cross so you would no longer bear the curse of God (see Gal. 3:13). This is why the Holy Spirit does not convict you of sins committed by your family members and those in your bloodline.

In other words, though demonic assignments may feel like Deuteronomic curses, they are not. It breaks my heart when I meet believers who think God has something against them as a result of their parents' sin. Often they are disconnected from the heart of the Father, struggle with rejection, and feel as though God is not pleased with them. This is why we need to be careful with our language—the phrase "generational curse" does not refer to the curses from God outlined in Deuteronomy. It simply refers to the reality that, as believers, we are still vulnerable to demonic assignments. These assignments are released by familiar spirits who attack each generation within our family at the same points of weakness.

THE FUNDAMENTALS OF STRONGHOLDS: MIND, WILL, AND EMOTIONS

Once they have gained access to our lives, demons begin to systematically go after our mind, will, and emotions. Although all three elements of the soul are equally susceptible to demonic influence, I have found that the mind is often the first target as well as the primary battleground. When the enemy is mounting an attack, lies based on our experiences begin to dominate and reshape our thought life. Next, our will and emotions become involved and fall to the onslaught. We choose to believe the lies and then act or react accordingly, damaging our hearts through sin. This process constitutes a stronghold. Simply put, a stronghold exists when a demonic spirit has the ability to consistently speak a lie and provoke a negative or sinful behavioral response in us.

> A stronghold exists when a demonic spirit has the ability to consistently speak a lie and provoke a negative or sinful behavioral response in us.

Here is an example we encounter all the time in the ministry of deliverance: Let's say a young woman experienced the trauma of sexual abuse as a child. When that happened, the enemy lied to her. He told her what happened was her fault and that she was worth nothing. Once she accepted the lies, she exercised her will and started to make choices accordingly. She became promiscuous and engaged in self-harm. The damage this inflicted on her emotions created a trigger the enemy could use against her constantly. Any time she felt shame, pain, or rejection, she responded by acting out sinfully. The lies that entered through her trauma were used by demons to control her will and emotions.

Some variation of this pattern is present in every stronghold. A lie comes to mind, our damaged emotions are triggered, and we react by engaging in sinful behaviors. While all three of these components working together constitute a stronghold, the lie is the root of the bondage. Habits of sin such as addiction, slander, anger, lying, jealousy, etc. can always be traced back to a certain point in time when a demonic lie first entered our mind.

> The lie is the root of the bondage.

And these root lies often end up supporting numerous, interconnecting strongholds. Remember the parable of the sower and the seed? If we return to the analogy of the soul as a garden, we can illustrate this point simply. Picture your soul as a garden plot with three rows. Each row represents patterns of thought. The first row contains your thoughts about God—what you believe about Him, what you think He's really like, and so forth. The second row contains your thoughts about yourself, and the third row contains your thoughts about others. The enemy comes along and sows seeds into each of these rows. These seeds carry lies, accusations, doubts, fears, and bitterness. When we meditate on these demonic seeds and accept them as truth, we begin to cultivate them. The root lie burrows deep into the soil of our soul, and then it branches out. Other, smaller lies appear and begin forming secondary strongholds. Soon we have a mass of interconnected strongholds, all producing the fruits of unrighteousness. These secondary strongholds usually need to be torn down before we can deal with the root lie.

DISCERNING THE STRONG MAN

When a strong man, fully armed, guards his own house, his possessions are undisturbed. But when someone stronger than he attacks him and overpowers him, he takes away from him all his armor on which he had relied and distributes his plunder. He who is not with Me is against Me; and he who does not gather with Me, scatters (Luke 11:21-23).

In the parable of the sower and the seed, Jesus compared the attack of the enemy to weeds in the garden of the human soul. Here, He gives us another analogy. Every stronghold in our lives is guarded by a "strong man." According to these verses, unless we deal with the strong man, we will not be able to successfully walk through deliverance and into freedom. This point is more directly emphasized in Matthew 12:29, where Jesus asks, "Or how can anyone enter the strong man's house and carry off his property, unless he first binds the strong man? And then he will plunder his house."

The strong man is the demonic spirit associated with the root lie in our souls. As we consistently agree with this lie, the strong man constructs a stronghold within our mind, will, and emotions and uses this to permanently oppress and control us. It does not do so alone, however. Demons work interactively to strengthen each other and prepare the way for other demonic spirits to gain access to our lives. Typically, each strong man has numerous servant spirits operating under it to create and maintain the stronghold.

> The strong man is the demonic spirit associated with the root lie in our souls.

In order to bind the strong man in the deliverance process, we need to discern its identity by examining patterns of sin and weakness in our lives and the lives of our family. (As we mentioned earlier, strongholds are often generational.) Unfortunately, this process of discernment has led to some confusion within the Church. Many believers have mistaken the effects produced by a particular demon for the demon itself. When the Word of God mentions a demonic spirit, such as "the spirit of fear" (2 Tim. 1:7 NKJV), it is referring to the ability of that spirit to produce fear. We should not conclude that the name of the demon is "fear."

Others are under the impression that they have to know a demon's name in order to command it to leave. However, I believe we should avoid all teachings on deliverance that require we know the name of a demon before we cast it out. The Bible only specifically names two fallen angels—Lucifer and Apollyon (see Isa. 14:12; Rev. 9:11). No other demons are singled out by name in the Scriptures. While there are those who believe the demoniac narrative in the gospel of Mark demonstrates the necessity of learning a spirit's name, I think this is a misinterpretation of the text. When Jesus was confronted by a demonized man in the country of the Gerasenes, He commanded the evil spirits to leave.

> *Seeing Jesus from a distance, he ran up and bowed down before Him; and shouting with a loud voice, he said, "What business do we have with each other, Jesus, Son of the Most High God? I implore You by God, do not torment me!" For He had been saying to him, "Come out of the man, you unclean spirit!"* (Mark 5:6-8)

The first thing we should notice is the authority the demons exercised over this man. They did not leave! When He saw this, Jesus asked the man a question:

> *And He was asking him, "What is your name?" And he said to Him, "My name is Legion; for we are many"* (Mark 5:9).

I do not believe Jesus was talking to the demons at this point (although they responded to His question). He had seen their authority, and in response He highlighted the issue of the man's agreement with their presence and activity. This man was so wrapped up in his identity as a demoniac that the spirits were free to talk through him at will; he no longer knew who he was. With one simple question, Jesus revealed the belief system ensnaring his identity and the demonic agreement within his soul. This agreement needed to be broken before the spirits would leave.

When viewed in this light, Mark 5 teaches us the importance of uncovering the root lie in the deliverance process. It does not teach us to dialogue with lying spirits and learn their names. The Lord is above such requirements, and He has given us the authority to cast out demons in His name.

Once we have identified the strong man/stronghold, we must figure out how and when it entered our lives and developed. Walking in freedom hinges upon our ability to fully deal with the root of the problem (the foundational lie we have believed). We do this by speaking and agreeing with truth. This may sound simple, but the process can be lengthy. It takes determination and emotional strength to push past the pain, the memories, and the lies within our soul in order to get at the root. And it is not enough to simply recite the truth; empty words do not have power. Instead, we need the anointing of the Holy Spirit to escort us into an encounter with the One who is true and exposes and destroys every work of darkness (see 1 John 5:18-20).

THREE LEVELS OF DEMONIC INFLUENCE

When we begin the deliverance process, we need to first evaluate the severity of the demonic bondage. Some lies are more easily uprooted than others, and some strongholds take more time and ministry to dismantle than others. Knowing the strength of the enemy will help us walk through the appropriate process. The first step in the evaluation is discerning whether or not there is an actual stronghold in operation. It is very common for believers to confuse temptation and warfare with strongholds. All three can cause emotional turmoil, but only one requires deliverance ministry.

We all experience warfare on a regular basis; the enemy assaults our mind and emotions and tries to trap us in lies and sin. When this happens, we typically just need someone to encourage us as we reject the lies and align our souls with the truth. The same principle applies to temptation. We all experience temptation, but that does not mean we are actively sinning and under the influence of a stronghold. It simply means we must stand firm and resist the enemy until he flees (see James 4:7). However, if the enemy is able to regularly control our behavior, then we probably have a stronghold and do need deliverance ministry.

The Bible does not directly state there are levels or degrees of demonic bondage, but several stories and verses in the New Testament seem to back up this observation. In Luke, Jesus warns His disciples about engaging in deliverance ministry when the person is not ready to receive truth and freedom.

> *When the unclean spirit goes out of a man, it passes through waterless places seeking rest, and not finding any, it says, "I will return to my house from which I came." And when it comes, it finds it swept and put in order. Then it goes and takes along seven other spirits more evil than itself, and they go in and live there; and the last state of that man becomes worse than the first* (Luke 11:24-26).

He specifically says "the last state of that man becomes worse"—in other words, not all experiences of demonic oppression are the same. Some are worse than others. We can draw this same conclusion through simple observation—the young woman who struggles with self-hatred and feels depressed when she looks in the mirror is probably not experiencing the same degree of oppression as the young man who is tripping on LSD and supernaturally breaking the handcuffs restraining him.

When I first began training others in deliverance ministry, I asked God for a simple way to help believers identify the severity of the demonic bondage in an individual's life. This prayer led me to outline three different levels of demonic influence. The first level of demonic influence is oppression. Everyone encounters this to one degree or another. It can be as small as a nagging accusation about your appearance ("you look fat"), or as big as physical sickness. Regardless of how it manifests, oppression is simply the resistance of the evil one. It is the everyday warfare we face as believers living in enemy territory. In fact, this level of attack is the most common among believers.

> Oppression is simply the
> resistance of the evil one.

I am convinced the western church has developed a distorted view of oppression. We have bought in to the lie that Christianity is about our comfort and security, and so we are shocked when we become targets of the enemy's attack. When we feel oppressed, we go running to the nearest conference, inner-healing ministry, or deliverance ministry rather than operating in our God-given authority and using the spiritual weapons available to us. I can't tell you how many times I have had some version of the following dialogue:

"Please pray for me; I am so depressed."

"Have you read your Bible this week?"

"No."

"Have you prayed in the last few days?"

"No."

"When was the last time you worshiped?"

"It's just been too hard."

"You haven't read your Bible, prayed, or worshiped? No wonder you're depressed! You're making me depressed!" When we are experiencing oppression, we need to learn to exercise the disciplines of our faith until we achieve breakthrough.

According to Peter, "His divine power has granted to us everything pertaining to life and godliness" (2 Pet. 1:3). We have access to divine power on the inside; we have literally been given everything we need to walk in godliness and experience life. No one else should shoulder the primary burden of our personal warfare. This doesn't mean we can never ask for help. As members of the Body, we want to come alongside one another and offer support and encouragement during difficult seasons. It can be helpful to have someone walk with us through repentance, forgiveness, and renouncing the lies we have believed. But we need to discern the line between reaching out in a healthy way for help and exhibiting codependency in our reliance upon the ministry of others.

> A person who is tormented is
> significantly deceived and unable
> to live according to the truth.

The second level of demonic influence is torment. A person who is oppressed may not *feel* like reading their Bible, praying, or worshiping, but they are capable of these activities and will eventually achieve breakthrough if they persevere. However, a person who is tormented is unable to read their Bible, pray, and worship. The stronghold in their life is so overwhelming that they are significantly deceived and unable to live according to the truth. When they attempt to align themselves with the Word of God or practice normal Christian disciplines, they often experience disruptive demonic manifestations. What does this look like? Some people may feel severe confusion, depression, or anger when they meditate on the Scriptures. Others may experience physical manifestations in a corporate worship setting, such as fainting, vomiting, panic attacks, violent behavior, and speaking with other voices. When a demon is able to speak through an individual or throw them to the ground, it is a good sign they are suffering from torment.

Usually a person suffering from demonic torment has a history of abuse or trauma. Perhaps they were molested as a child or had a near-death experience. Perhaps they were heavily involved in addiction and substance abuse or practiced the occult before they accepted Christ. Regardless, the strongholds operating in their life have much deeper roots than the strongholds affecting a person struggling with level-one oppression. This person will need the prayers and ministry of other believers in order to break the hold of the enemy on their life.

It is important to note that a believer can be tormented. In Matthew 18 Jesus tells the parable of the unforgiving servant and warns the disciples that their heavenly Father will deliver them to the tormentors unless they forgive their brothers (see Matt. 18:32-35). In other words, even Christians can give demons legal access to portions of their lives. How many believers do you know who are struggling with addiction, unable to read their Bibles and pray, suffering from debilitating depression, etc.? Though they have accepted Christ, they have not yet dealt with the issues from their past. It will take a combination of inner healing and deliverance to help them identify and uproot the strongholds that are preventing them from living a normal Christian life.

Let me illustrate this point with a story. I was once asked to visit a woman suffering from incredible demonic torment. She was a Christian, and for many years had worked with senior leaders in the Body of Christ. Just five years prior to my visit she was on fire for God. But when I walked into her living room, I immediately felt a thick, dark demonic presence. The woman was sitting on her couch, pulling out her hair and picking at open sores on her face. She was diagnosed with schizophrenia and bipolar disorder and was on numerous medications. What had happened to her? As we began to walk through inner healing and deliverance, I discovered she was led to believe she was the daughter of Satan. Apparently, spirits of accusation had attacked her and convinced her she had committed the unforgivable sin. She would stand in front of the mirror and see her own reflection transform as demons materialized and told her she was no longer a child of God. Over time we began to break the power of this lie and deal with the emotional wounds created by the constant abuse of the demonic spirits. Today, this woman is free from torment and on the path of total recovery. She no longer takes medication, and her relationship with God is restored and more vibrant than ever.

> Only a person who has never
> accepted Jesus Christ as their Savior
> can experience domination.

The third level of demonic influence is domination. A born-again Christian cannot be dominated by demonic spirits. Only a person who has never accepted Jesus Christ as their Savior can experience this level of demonic activity. Domination can occur in one of two ways: either an individual actively invited demons to enter them and take control (through participation in false religions or occult rituals) or they experienced a mental breakdown due to severe emotional and physical pain. This is why we see so many cases of demonic domination in psychiatric hospitals, prisons, and homeless ministries.

I purposefully use the term *domination* rather than *possession* because I do not believe a person is ever fully and utterly possessed by demons. Even in severe cases, the individual's will is still involved. In Mark 5 the demoniac from the country of the Gerasenes chose to approach Jesus; he exercised the ability to run toward God rather than away from Him, even though he was under the influence of numerous demonic spirits.

Unless they sincerely desire to be free, I will not walk through deliverance with a dominated individual. They may ask for prayer and then proceed to manipulate and attack the ministry team. This is why great caution and discernment are needed. The example we saw in Mark 5 provides a helpful guideline for determining whether or not an individual sincerely wants to turn to God: if they run up to us and ask to be saved, it is a good sign they are genuinely ready for salvation and deliverance.

In the next chapter we will look at the practical steps of deliverance ministry. These steps will help us safely navigate ministry times, but our faith and confidence do not rest in models and formulas. Neither do they rest in our knowledge and experience or personal spiritual gifting. They rest in God alone.

CHAPTER SIX

OPERATING IN DELIVERANCE MINISTRY

THE CALL TO DELIVERANCE MINISTRY

In Matthew 6, in the midst of His great Sermon on the Mount discourse, Jesus instructed His disciples regarding prayer. We are all familiar with these verses. "Our Father" is one of the few passages most people can recite, whether or not they are believers. But have you ever considered the implication of the final request found in this prayer? "And do not lead us into temptation, but deliver us from evil" (Matt. 6:13). Jesus incorporated deliverance ministry into His model prayer. This is how He wanted His disciples—all of His disciples—to pray regularly. We are told to ask the Father to keep us from falling into demonic temptation, and to deliver us from evil strongholds operating in our life.

When we read the gospels, we see deliverance was a normal part of Jesus's ministry. Again and again we are told He delivered those tormented by evil spirits (see Matt. 4:24; Mark 5:15; Luke 6:18). He commissioned the twelve and the seventy to cast out demons as they proclaimed the kingdom of God (see Mark 6:7; Luke 10:17).

> Deliverance is not a ministry reserved for the spiritual elite.

Heal the sick, raise the dead, cleanse the lepers, cast out demons. Freely you received, freely give (Matthew 10:8).

I love the principle of receiving and giving contained in this verse. Deliverance is not a ministry reserved for the spiritual elite. It flows freely from the heart of God to all His children, and as we have received we are empowered to give. Freedom is meant to overflow and multiply in the kingdom of God. In fact, this ministry is so foundational to our faith that Jesus included it in His final commissioning of the disciples before the ascension.

These signs will accompany those who have believed: in My name they will cast out demons, they will speak with new tongues; they will pick up serpents, and if they drink any deadly poison, it will not hurt them; they will lay hands on the sick, and they will recover (Mark 16:17-18).

Deliverance is part of the general calling of believers. We are all anointed to cast out demons, set the captives free, and manifest the power of the kingdom to those in need. However, there is a lack of knowledge and understanding concerning this ministry prevalent in the Body of Christ today. My desire in this chapter is to share practical and pastoral insights from my experience. With a healthy paradigm and some basic scriptural principles, we can all step into this element of our calling.

When I first began practicing deliverance, I viewed the ministry as a power struggle: "Come out, devil, or I'm coming in after you!" This is the paradigm of deliverance for many in the Body of Christ today. However, this approach can produce a lot of negative side effects. I have seen some terrible and traumatic deliverance sessions where people turned unnatural colors, levitated, projectile-vomited blood, and inflicted harm on themselves and others. I have seen ministers engage in lengthy power struggles with demons, and in the process trample over the dignity of the person receiving prayer. But none of this is necessary. When we are equipped to ask the right questions and evaluate the timing of the ministry, deliverance is a simple and safe process. I have overseen the deliverance ministry at IHOP-KC for the last six years, and in that time we have experienced no violent manifestations during ministry sessions. My heart in writing this book is to prevent you from making the same mistakes I made as a young man!

It is my conviction that we must receive revelation pertaining to deliverance in our personal devotional life first and foremost. God wants to lead us through our own journey of freedom as we communicate with Him in the secret place before He releases us to lead others down the same path. This is why the prayer, "deliver us from evil," begins with addressing the Father. As we walk through foundational information regarding the practice of deliverance ministry, I encourage you to maintain a dialogue with the Father. Ask Him to show you places in your life where He wants to bring freedom, and lean in to Him for wisdom regarding the practical application of these principles.

A NOTE ON AUTHORITY

It is important to recognize the difference between walking in the authority to cast out demons and confronting principalities or Satan himself. The call to deliverance ministry is for everyone in the Body of Christ; we have all been given authority over certain levels of the demonic hierarchy. However, as we saw when we examined what the Scriptures have to say about Satan, there are levels of demonic power where we need to exercise great caution and humility.

Many people who believe we are empowered to confront *every* demonic power point to the passage in Luke where the seventy return and report on the success of their ministry:

> *The seventy returned with joy, saying, "Lord, even the demons are subject to us in Your name." And He said to them, "I was watching Satan fall from heaven like lightning. Behold, I have given you authority to tread on serpents and scorpions, and over all the power of the enemy, and nothing will injure you. Nevertheless do not rejoice in this, that the spirits are subject to you, but rejoice that your names are recorded in heaven"* (Luke 10:17-20).

I have heard believers state that when we cast out demons, Satan falls in the spirit. This is a common interpretation of the passage, but I advocate a different interpretation. When Jesus speaks, He is actually warning and rebuking the disciples. Satan fell due to his pride, and Jesus does not want His followers to make the same mistake and stumble into pride over their spiritual authority. This is why He tells them not to rejoice when demonic spirits are subject to them. It is important to walk in humility when we engage in spiritual warfare—and this includes recognizing that when we confront a disembodied spirit operating through an individual, we are not directly confronting Satan.

This does not mean believers are never authorized to wrestle against principalities and other high-ranking demonic spirits. There are proper ways to engage in higher levels of spiritual warfare, but they usually involve the corporate Body. We will look at the role of the Church in overcoming principalities and powers in a later chapter.

While we need to recognize the limitations of our authority over demonic spirits, we also need to recognize the limitations of our authority over the person we are walking through the deliverance process. We cannot override the free will of another human soul. At the end of the day, the person has to desire and choose freedom. This is actually the first question I ask someone when they approach me for ministry: "Do you want to be free? Are you willing to make changes in your life in order to maintain your freedom?"

> We cannot override the free will of another human soul. At the end of the day, the person has to desire and choose freedom.

Sadly, for many the answer to this question is no. They like the idea of freedom, but don't like the things they have to give up in order to be free. People are accustomed to their sin; they want to hold on to their pet insecurities and secret comforts. If I try to walk someone like this through deliverance, it will be at best an exercise in futility, and at worst an open door for even greater bondage (see Luke 11:24-26). It is dangerous to use deliverance ministry as a quick fix to deal with the negative consequences of sin. People who do so will show up for prayer again and again but never receive breakthrough. Eventually, their heart will harden and they will end up in greater bondage. If an individual is unwilling or unable to take the necessary steps to obtain victory and break the power of the stronghold in their life, than they are not ready for deliverance ministry.

Let's return to the analogy of the soul as a garden for a moment. I can help someone uproot strongholds, and I can sow seeds of truth, but I cannot cultivate those seeds for them. Only they can choose to reject lies, meditate on truth, and shut the door on patterns of sin. Before you begin praying with someone, talk to them and find out whether or not their garden is prepared to receive the seed of truth. Are they willing to do the work of preparation? Are they in an environment that will support or hinder their transformation? Ultimately, we are all as free as we choose to be.

> We are all as free as we choose to be.

FIVE-STEP DELIVERANCE MODEL

In this book I want to present a basic model for ministering deliverance to someone with level-one oppression. If an individual has experienced attack in the form of fear, depression, immorality, etc., then they may need to have someone pray with them in order to break off the oppression. I have found this model very effective in empowering believers to receive and maintain freedom. It works equally well in private ministry settings and altar ministry settings. However, I do not recommend following this model when praying with someone who is experiencing torment or domination (levels two and three of demonic influence). In most cases such a person will need more care and assistance than you can provide, and should be referred to a local church leader or deliverance ministry.

I refer to the five-step deliverance model as the Five Cs:

1. Communicate

2. Cancel

3. Cleanse

4. Command

5. Counsel

Communicate

Step one is *communication*. You need to talk to the person seeking prayer and find out what is going on. It is important to approach this step and every step in the process as a partnership. You are standing with a brother or sister as they confront the enemy and cast him out; you are partnering with them, not doing something to them. As you begin to ask them about their circumstances and need for prayer, make sure they are engaging in the process. They have to want freedom and be willing to actively pursue it. If it feels as though they are depending on you to do all the work, it is better to postpone the deliverance. Otherwise, you will end up enabling codependent patterns of ministry where believers rely on ministers to keep the enemy at bay rather than owning their issues, taking responsibility, and growing in maturity.

> You are partnering with them, not
> doing something to them.

Start out the communication process by asking why they feel the need for deliverance. Ask if they are aware of any sin or unforgiveness in their life. (You may need to explain how sin and unforgiveness give the enemy access to our lives.) Keep in mind they may simply be feeling the effects of warfare. Exercise discernment as you listen in order to determine whether there is an actual stronghold in place. As they continue to share, ask follow-up questions. If you receive a word of knowledge or simply sense there is more going on than what they have articulated, present it to them as a suggestion or a question: "I feel like there may be an addiction involved. Is that something you struggle with?" "I think we may need to break off fear. Does that resonate with you?" This is a safety mechanism to prevent psychological damage. If a believer is told they need deliverance from a specific issue when they do not, they may begin to doubt their freedom in that area and ultimately open the door to the enemy.

We have all heard of the power of suggestion. I have seen its effects many times. A believer responds to an altar call for physical healing, others gather around them to pray, and suddenly someone starts proclaiming loudly, "I bind every spirit of witchcraft! I break every generational curse!" These things are included in the prayer for healing as though they are fact, and the individual receiving prayer is never given the chance to confirm or deny anything. They may be a visitor at the church, or may not be familiar with spiritual warfare and deliverance.

Either way, they walk away thinking they have problems they don't. Our words are powerful, so we must be careful in the way we approach the topic of demonic oppression.

You may need to take authority over any demons that manifest during the time of communication. The interview process requires complete attention and cooperation, and there are many ways a demonic spirit can try to disrupt it. The person might start to physically manifest, or they might lose the ability to focus and think clearly, or they might start to exhibit a different personality. This is a good sign the enemy is trying to prevent you from getting the information you need. Simply command every unclean spirit to submit to the name of Jesus, and gently encourage the person to take control of their body and mind. This should not be difficult if the person is ready and willing to receive ministry.

Notice that I use the phrase "take authority over" rather than "bind." It is very common in charismatic denominations to hear believers use the language of binding in deliverance ministry. This language is inspired by two specific passages. In Mark 3:27 Jesus states, "But no one can enter the strong man's house and plunder his property unless he first binds the strong man, and then he will plunder his house." While this verse does illustrate a principle of deliverance, it is told in the form of a parable. In other words, we are not meant to interpret the action of binding literally. In Matthew 16:19, Jesus declares to Peter and the disciples, "whatever you bind on earth shall have been bound in heaven, and whatever you loose on earth shall have been loosed in heaven." Although the language of binding seems to apply literally here, it has nothing to do with deliverance ministry. In fact, nowhere in Scripture are we commanded to bind demonic spirits. I doubt an angel descends from heaven with a rope every time someone prays, "I bind you."

Why then does the language of binding work? Even though the terminology is not strictly accurate, the spirit realm understands what we mean when we say, "I bind you in the name of Jesus." We are exercising our authority and compelling the demon to submit to us and cease manifesting. God does not penalize us for technicalities. In the same way He does not require us to know a demon's name before we cast it out, so He does not wait for us to use the correct phrase before backing up our words with His power and authority. For years I used the language of binding, and despite its inaccuracy it was very effective. However, I now prefer to say, "I take authority over you in the name of Jesus."

Cancel

Step two is *cancel*. If I sign an agreement giving you access to my private property, I can't turn around and make you leave the property. You have legal permission to remain. The only way I can get you to leave is by cancelling my agreement. This scenario illustrates how demons operate in the spirit. The issue of deliverance is the issue of agreement. Demons will not leave until we take away their legal permission. We do this by repenting of our sin, forgiving those who have sinned against us, and renouncing our partnership/agreement with the demons operating in our lives. Once this is done, we can kick the enemy off our property.

> The issue of deliverance is
> the issue of agreement.

Here is a generic prayer model that may be helpful. Make sure you explain the importance of repenting for sin, forgiving

others, and renouncing the enemy. Then have them repeat after you:

> *Jesus, I believe You are the Son of God. I believe You died on the cross for my sins and rose again from the dead. I confess You as my Lord and Savior. I repent of all my sins (list specific sins here). I forgive all who have wronged or harmed me. I lay down all resentment, hatred, and rebellion. In particular, I forgive (name specific individuals here). I also forgive myself for all the sins that I have committed against You and others. I renounce the demonic spirits that I have allowed into my life. I renounce the demonic lies I have believed (list specific lies here). Lord, I ask You to forgive me and cleanse me by Your precious blood. Right now I accept Your love and forgiveness.*

Make sure they repent of all their known sins and forgive everyone who has wronged them. Do not assume the person has been completely honest with you about these issues. We are all insecure when it comes to revealing the darkness in our hearts! If it is taking a long time for them to list their sins, or if the deliverance process stalls at a later step, revisit the discussion of repentance and forgiveness and ask them whether they are still holding on to something.

Usually people only think of the men and women they need to forgive, but so many of us have suppressed bitterness and resentment toward God. I often begin by asking the person receiving ministry if they are angry at God for any reason. This can be a very effective way of exposing the hidden bitterness and resentment in their heart. While God is able to set us free even if we have not literally forgiven everyone in our lives, there is a clear scriptural warning concerning the bondage we will experience if we fail to release offense held against God, ourselves, or others (see Matt. 18:21-22, 34-35). When an individual is walking through forgiveness, have them mention each person by name; this is so much more powerful than a blanket statement of forgiveness! Our hearts are impacted by our voices, and we will actually experience emotional release when we declare forgiveness with our mouths.

> Our hearts are impacted by our voices, and we will actually experience emotional release when we declare forgiveness with our mouths.

Cleanse

Step three is *cleanse*. It is important to reclaim enemy territory in the soul. A time of cleansing and healing prayer will begin to replace lies with truth and lay new foundations where enemy strongholds once stood. You are not seeking to completely resolve issues of pain here, because that is usually a longer inner-healing process. Instead, you want to make sure the issues have all been surrendered to God, and then invite the Holy Spirit to begin healing the person from the effects of their sin, wounds, and strongholds.

During this time of prayer you want to replace lies with truth, declare God's forgiveness over them, and wash them in His love. Remind the person of the lies they renounced during the second step, and prompt them to ask God for His truth. Speak that truth back over them and ask the Holy Spirit to lead them into even greater revelation and freedom. Speak words of forgiveness and cleansing; let them know they are spotless before God. Also take time to declare His love over them and speak words of prophetic encouragement and blessing.

In his letter to the Ephesians, Paul speaks of the power of the Word of God to wash us (see Eph. 5:26). When you partner with Christ in this ministry, you are actually building the faith of the person receiving prayer. They are receiving truth and being prepared for the next step—warfare. It is helpful to have them join you in speaking truth toward the end of the time of cleansing prayer. Invite them to declare who they are in Christ. This equips them to resist the counterattack of the enemy and maintain their freedom.

Command

Step four is *command.*

> *Just then there was a man in their synagogue with an unclean spirit; and he cried out, saying, "What business do we have with each other, Jesus of Nazareth? Have You come to destroy us? I know who You are—the Holy One of God!" And Jesus rebuked him, saying,* **"Be quiet, and come out of him!"** *...They were all amazed, so that they debated among themselves, saying, "What is this? A new teaching with authority! He commands even the unclean spirits, and they obey Him"* (Mark 1:23-25, 27).

Once we have cancelled the legal right for a demon to remain, deliverance is very simple. Jesus shows us what to do in the gospel of Mark: He silences the spirit and then commands it to leave. There is no need for us to shout or move around in a dramatic manner. Demons respond to the authority of Jesus, not our volume or theatricality.

Begin by letting the person know you are entering into a time of warfare. Tell them you will command the demons to leave, and then invite them to join you by repeating your prayers. In this way you are partnering with them to cast the enemy out and simultaneously training them to resist any counterattack. Here is an example of how you might pray:

> *I agree with the prayers and confession of (insert their name here). In the name of Jesus, I command every unclean spirit to go. Your power is broken; you will not manifest or humiliate this person in any way.*

Then invite them to repeat after you:

> *In the name of Jesus, I command every spirit associated with the stronghold of (list the specific strongholds here) to go.*

Do not mention any strongholds unless they have already been discussed and acknowledged during the initial step of communication. You do not want the person to think they have more demons than they actually do!

There may be a small manifestation as the demons leave, such as coughing, sneezing, burping, yawning, or vomiting. However, none of these need to happen in order for deliverance to take place. Regardless of whether or not there is physical evidence, we believe by faith that every spirit is under the authority of Jesus Christ and must obey those who proclaim His name. However, if the person begins to manifest in a violent and alarming way or loses consciousness, command the spirit to be silent and end the deliverance session. Explain that they are exhibiting signs of level-two demonic influence and will need to be referred to a leader or senior deliverance minister.

Counsel

Step five is *counsel*. Once you feel the oppression has lifted, confirm this with the person receiving deliverance and then end by praying and prophesying over them. Declare again their freedom in Christ and bless them with the presence of the Holy Spirit. Finally, have a conversation about the need for consecration in their life. Encourage them to maintain their freedom by closing the doors to the enemy and counsel them appropriately concerning issues of sin. Remind them to read the Word of God and fill themselves with truth concerning who He is and who they are to Him. This will prevent the enemy from returning and establishing a new stronghold within them (see Luke 11:24-26; John 5:14).

THE NEED FOR INNER HEALING

While counseling is the fifth and final step of the deliverance model, it is not the end of the journey for the person receiving ministry. Even with the enemy gone, there are often wounds that need healing. If we do not help the mind and emotions recover, then demonic spirits will simply return at a later date and establish new strongholds. For this reason I believe inner healing needs to be incorporated into the general philosophy of deliverance. I am not going to address the subject of inner healing here, but I strongly encourage you to pursue training and experience in this subject before you embark on deliverance ministry.

DISCERNING THE TIMING OF
DELIVERANCE MINISTRY

Now that we have looked at a general deliverance model, let's examine how to appropriately handle a ministry situation in a corporate context. It is not uncommon in large worship services or conference settings to encounter individuals exhibiting signs of demonic influence. However, we should not assume a person is ready for deliverance just because they are manifesting a demon. This is an important point. We must be led by the Lord and use wisdom and discernment when deciding on the timing of ministry. Even the apostle Paul waited several days before commanding the spirit of divination to leave a Macedonian slave girl who was harassing him (see Acts 16:16-18).

> We should not assume a person is ready for deliverance just because they are manifesting a demon.

One of the crucial factors to consider is the dignity of the individual. I have been in corporate worship settings where a group of people gathered around an individual, yelling "Come out!" or "In the name of Jesus, every foul and perverted spirit must go now!" This is traumatic to the person receiving prayer. Not only are people yelling at them, but their struggles are being uncovered and broadcast to the entire room. This is never a good way to walk someone through deliverance. With this in mind, let's walk through the practical steps we should take when an individual manifests a demon in a corporate meeting.

The first thing you should do is observe your surroundings and determine what is causing the demon to manifest. Usually it is one of two things—the atmosphere and anointing in the room are stirring up demonic resistance, or your individual anointing is uncovering the enemy as you pray for the person. Ask yourself the question, "When did this individual begin exhibiting signs of oppression and torment? Was it during worship, or was it when I began praying for them during an altar call?" If the person is responding to your individual anointing, stop praying for them. You do not want to stir up demonic activity that will humiliate them and distract the entire room. Instead, consider having a conversation with them about setting up a private deliverance appointment at a later date.

If the demon is responding to the corporate atmosphere, then you need to remove the person from the room completely. (Remember, we are talking about disruptive, demonic manifestations that are distracting others and embarrassing or tormenting the individual.) If you are in a position of authority at the church or conference, you can ask the person directly to leave the room with you and one or two other prayer ministers. However, if you are a guest without a recognized position of authority in the service, you will need to find a leader or usher to assist you. (You should not walk someone through deliverance by yourself. For your own safety and the safety of the person receiving prayer, make sure there are a few individuals involved.)

Once they have been removed from the corporate context, the next step is to take authority over the spirit so that the manifestation ceases. Use the name of Jesus and command the demon to be silent. Remember, the person has the ability to exercise their will and cooperate with you. Do not buy in to the lie that the demon has total authority over them. Sit them down, look them in the eye, use their name, and gently tell them to exercise their will and stop the manifestations.

Encourage them by speaking truth in the moment: "This spirit does not have complete control over you. I know you do not want this. God loves you and He wants to set you free. You have the ability to take control of your body now." Continue to command the spirit to be quiet, but do not cast it out. At this point you only have the authority to silence the demon. You cannot cast it out until you have walked the person through deliverance and they have cancelled their agreement.

If they continue to manifest in disruptive and violent ways, then you know they are still in agreement with their bondage and simply want attention. At this point you should walk away. Do not launch into a deliverance session or attempt to get more information by dialoguing with the demonic spirits. However, if they respond positively and the manifestations stop, you should enter into the first step of the deliverance model—communication. There are several things you want to find out. What level of demonic influence is present in their life? How strong is their foundational knowledge of God? What is their history with this particular stronghold? Are they ready to make the necessary sacrifices and changes to maintain freedom?

Based on the information you receive, you can then determine whether to walk them through deliverance immediately, set up a later ministry appointment, or refer them to church leadership. I do not recommend engaging in deliverance right away if the person is struggling with anything more than level-one demonic influence. If they are unable to read the Bible, pray, or worship, they are probably dealing with a bigger issue than can be handled in an impromptu ministry session. You might be able to aggressively attack the stronghold and cast the demon out, but without the proper support system and foundational knowledge of God, they will not be able to maintain their freedom.

In the next chapters I want to take a step back and look at the bigger picture. Deliverance ministry may be the frontline in the battle against demonic deception and bondage, but it is not the whole war. If we are serious in our pursuit of the kingdom, we will inevitably face the enemy's assault against our environment, our knowledge of God, our identity, and our corporate calling as the Body of Christ. Arming ourselves with understanding and discernment concerning these things will prevent us from becoming needless casualties and equip us to fight for the freedom of others as well.

CHAPTER SEVEN

DEMONIC WORLD SYSTEMS

HAVE YOU EVER STOPPED TO CONSIDER THE FACT THAT YOUR environment primarily functions under the authority of darkness? There are specific social and governmental structures you encounter on a daily basis that serve to further the agenda of the enemy. In fact, we live in a culture filled with demonic systems of rejection set in place to wound and confuse humanity. The enemy is a counterfeiter, and he runs his kingdom using the governing principles of heaven. Just as God searches for men and women fully submitted to Him and then anoints them with authority to implement His plans and purposes, so the enemy partners with men and women to achieve his aims. When someone yields their life to demonic lies, principalities anoint them with favor and authority to carry out demonic agendas.

We see these agendas manifest in every arena. In the last few decades, leaders in the Body of Christ have identified seven different subsets of the general culture where the battle for the nations is being waged—economy, education, family, government, media, religion, and sports/entertainment.[1] This list is a helpful tool when it comes to analyzing the culture we live in and the systematic attack of the enemy. I want to highlight his plans in just a few of these arenas. I believe we are in the midst of an unprecedented breakdown of the family unit and an all-out assault against parenting. By and large, our educational system has abandoned the idea of parents and extended family members as primary educators and caretakers. One of the negative effects of this approach is that it creates a breakdown between parents and children. Parents are anointed with God-given authority and insight to raise and train their children, but this authority is usurped when the children are isolated from their parents and exposed to other influences. How many of us first had the doors to sin and darkness opened in our lives as children and teens through peer pressure? When we suffer a deficit of relational connection, love, and acceptance in the family unit, we turn to others to fill that void—and often walk away from God in the process.

> We live in a culture filled with demonic systems of rejection set in place to wound and confuse humanity.

In the arena of government, the enemy is working to raise up corrupt and manipulative leaders. Ultimately, such leaders cause us to reject the ideas of government and authority altogether. When those in office are consumed by personal power struggles, the battle for status and influence, and the need to deceive their constituents, then we end up with populations eager to throw off all restraint and government. The problem is that God's kingdom operates through the principles of government. In fact, His kingdom is a theocracy—there is one divine ruler, and no one gets to vote! How many of us find ourselves thinking, "That sounds horrible!" in response to the above statement? We have been conditioned to reject our coming King because we cannot comprehend the existence of an absolute ruler who is perfectly just, infinitely good, and utterly humble. Who has ever seen a servant-king? Who has ever visited a kingdom founded on righteousness and justice? When have we ever seen the last made first and the first made last? When have we ever seen the meek exalted instead of exploited? When have we tasted the joy of submitting to a leader who rules in perfect humility? These things seem impossible, especially when we contrast them with our experiences of government. We need to be set free from our fear of authority so we can actually embrace the kingdom of God and cultivate hearts of submission and obedience rather than individualism and rebellion.

In the arena of the economy, we are inundated with the demonic messages of materialism. We are conditioned to go after the American Dream—the nice house, nice car, and nice job that ensure social status and personal comfort. This could not be more contrary to the call of the kingdom. Jesus invites us to lay our lives down, while the world tells us to take care of ourselves first and foremost. Jesus tells us to find our success and identity in our relationship with Him, while the world tells us to find our success in what we own, what we drive, and what we wear. We are constantly living in the tension between these two systems, feeling ourselves pulled in opposing directions and confused about what we really want. I am telling you, it's demonic.

In the arena of the entertainment industry, we see demonic systems of rejection that attack our self-worth. The messages our culture sends men and women about their identity and value are appalling. Vanity, materialism, and the opinions of others are exalted above everything. We are encouraged to obsess over physical beauty and cultural popularity, and our hearts pay the price. This is a far cry from what God calls beautiful in His kingdom. Humility, self-denial, purity, and all-consuming love for God and others—these are the true measure of a man or woman. But as long as we continue to measure ourselves against the standards of the culture and pursue worldly acceptance, we will fail to cultivate true beauty and open ourselves up to intense rejection.

> We cannot comprehend the existence of
> an absolute ruler who is perfectly just,
> infinitely good, and utterly humble.

As this brief overview of various demonic world systems reveals, we are surrounded by governmental, social, and cultural pressures to give in to the ways of the flesh and the lies of the enemy. Paul warns about the effect of this pressure in his letter to the Romans. In an earlier chapter we talked about the importance of dialoguing with the Holy Spirit in order to partner with His work of sanctification in our lives. But Paul has so much more to teach us about the Holy Spirit and the battle for the human soul!

For the mind set on the flesh is death, but the mind set on the Spirit is life and peace, because the mind set on the flesh is hostile toward God;

for it does not subject itself to the law of God, for it is not even able to do so (Romans 8:6-7).

In these verses Paul is talking about more than the battle against lust and immorality. He is describing the clash of two ways of life, two world systems—the flesh and the spirit.

For the flesh sets its desire against the Spirit, and the Spirit against the flesh; for these are in opposition to one another, so that you may not do the things that you please (Galatians 5:17).

> We are surrounded by governmental, social, and cultural pressures to give in to the ways of the flesh and the lies of the enemy.

To the degree we are in agreement with the flesh, we experience an internal war between body and spirit. This agreement is often unintentional or unnoticed—we simply adhere to the cultural norms around us without questioning how they measure up against the values of the Sermon on the Mount or the spiritual laws of the kingdom. But when we run after the things of the world and evaluate our lives according to the culture's standards of success, we are actually striving against the Holy Spirit within us.

As we begin to mature in our faith and learn to walk according to the spirit, we experience a different kind of conflict. We are no longer at war internally, but we find ourselves rejected by the world. Jesus Himself declared we would have trouble in the world (see John 16:33). He warned us not to love the world, and not to find our identity in it. Is it possible we struggle with oppression and depression in our lives due to our divided hearts? We must actively grow in our hatred of the world and embrace the trials that come with this stance if we want to experience the love, joy, and peace of the kingdom.

This is why there are so many verses in the New Testament reminding believers to expect rejection. Peter actually told the churches to anticipate suffering at the hands of those who did not understand their withdrawal from drunkenness, sensuality, lawlessness, idolatry, etc. (see 1 Pet. 4:1-4). It is common sense to expect conflict and rejection when we seek to live in a godly manner and oppose the spirit of the age. When our very lives confront the demonic power structures around us, we should not be surprised by the attack of the enemy. Losing sight of this will cause us to fall into the trap of operating within the world's systems just to avoid the pain of rejection.

THE WAR AGAINST THE KNOWLEDGE OF GOD

While Satan works to advance his agenda through numerous social and governmental structures, he simultaneously seeks to undermine individual believers in two primary areas—the knowledge of God and the revelation of our identity. In Matthew 22, Jesus was questioned by a lawyer concerning the greatest commandment. This was His response: "'You shall love the Lord your God with all your heart, and with all your soul, and with all your mind.' This is the great and foremost commandment. The second is like it, 'You shall love your neighbor as yourself'" (Matt. 22:37-39). When the enemy works to destroy our knowledge of God and our identity, he is effectively launching an attack against the two greatest commandments in our lives. We will spend the remainder of this chapter examining the knowledge of God, and look at the subject of identity in the next chapter.

> When our very lives confront the demonic power structures around us, we should not be surprised by the attack of the enemy.

Our thoughts concerning who God is and what He is like are the initial target for most demonic assignments. When we are saved, the Lord begins the process of sanctifying and healing our wounded minds and emotions. But the enemy constantly seeks to abort this process and prevent us from receiving the knowledge of God. I have seen this play out again and again in my years of deliverance ministry. Regardless of the issue, at some point the enemy crept in and sowed lies concerning God's nature: "He isn't good. He won't provide for you. He isn't powerful enough to save you. He is distant and disinterested."

I personally experienced an intense battle over the knowledge of God during my time at the Brownsville Revival. I was still a very new believer, and night after night I was inundated with messages on the holiness of God, the need for repentance, and the danger of grieving the Holy Spirit. Slowly my mind and heart were overtaken by fear, and I developed a performance-driven mentality. Although I was completely devoted to the things of the kingdom, it constantly seemed like I was falling short and failing. I remember feeling as though I was getting saved every week because the altar calls were all about getting rid of the sin in your life! I knew God loved me, but I didn't know He liked me.

Then I was introduced to a man named Steve Hill. This was not Steve Hill, the fiery evangelist and holiness preacher instrumental in leading the Brownsville Revival. It was a different man with the same name, a man who began to teach me about the Father's heart. He told me God liked me and invited me to experience the tender affections of the Lord. This was a radical paradigm shift in my life. Slowly my mind and emotions were transformed and set free as I encountered the knowledge of God's love and kindness.

> Our thoughts concerning who God is and what He is like are the initial target for most demonic assignments.

Before, I used to read verses like Isaiah 55:9 and think about how pathetic I was compared to God: "For as the heavens are higher than the earth, so are My ways higher than your ways and My thoughts than your thoughts." I never realized this verse was describing the Father's delight in mercy and compassion! Stop for a moment and ask yourself the question, "What do I enjoy?" For example, I really enjoy golf. In fact, I once had the opportunity to play golf with a pro, and the night before I was so excited I literally couldn't sleep. Now ask yourself, "What does God enjoy?" The prophet Micah gives us the incredible answer:

> *Who is a God like You, who pardons iniquity and passes over the rebellious act of the remnant of His possession? He does not retain His anger forever, because He delights in unchanging love* (Micah 7:18).

In the same way we look forward to a good book or movie, an exotic vacation, time with friends and family, a sporting event, or even a favorite dessert, God looks forward to loving us. It is His delight—His favorite thing. When this truth begins to penetrate our souls, it changes everything.

> I knew God loved me, but I
> didn't know He liked me.

However, when we lack this truth and instead possess distorted and broken views of God, a multitude of other evils fill our lives. Because we do not trust God's leadership, we are unable to trust other leaders. This can produce conflict, anxiety, and unsanctified independence among other things. We may struggle with finances or be crippled by the fear of losing our relationships or our health. We may even wrestle with issues of control and struggle to let others participate in our lives. Because we do not know how we are loved and valued by the Father, we are riddled with insecurity, jealousy, and the need to compete and compare. "Why are they so blessed, while I am struggling?" We are easily offended by small snubs, and quick to sense rejection in every situation. We may even wall ourselves off from others, determined to reject them before they have the chance to hurt us.

These are just a few examples of the mental, emotional, and relational damage produced by our distorted views of God. When we do not know Him as He really is, we become vulnerable to every kind of deception and bondage. For this reason I believe the greatest need within the Body of Christ today is the reclamation of the knowledge of God. Theologian A.W. Tozer sheds great insight on this dilemma in his book, *The Knowledge of the Holy*.

What comes into our minds when we think about God is the most important thing about us...and the most portentous fact about any man is not what he at a given time may say or do, but what he in his deep heart conceives God to be like. We tend by a secret law of the soul to move toward our mental image of God.[2]

> The first and most important step is to recognize our condition before Him.

When Paul described his apostolic mandate to the Corinthian church, he highlighted the demonic assignment against the minds of believers. His preaching and teaching were intended to dismantle every attack on the knowledge of God:

> *We are destroying speculations and every lofty thing raised up against the knowledge of God, and we are taking every thought captive to the obedience of Christ* (2 Corinthians 10:5).

This is not just an apostolic mandate. The Scriptures exhort us as individuals to guard our minds:

> *Set your mind on the things above, not on the things that are on earth* (Colossians 3:2).

> *Therefore, prepare your minds for action, keep sober in spirit, fix your hope completely on the grace to be brought to you at the revelation of Jesus Christ* (1 Peter 1:13).

We are called to actively dismantle every attack against the knowledge of God by focusing our mind's eye on things above. This is not a vague directive; there are practical steps we can take on a daily basis to fight for an increase of the knowledge of God in our lives. The first and most important step is to recognize our condition before Him. This sounds simple, but how many of us are actually going about our lives disconnected from the fear of the Lord? (When I refer to the fear of the Lord, I am talking about the reverence and awe we experience when we catch a glimpse of who God is and what He has done for us. It is not the fear of punishment or hell.) When we are reminded of His holiness and His majesty, we become aware of our own depravity and fallen condition. This revelation of our weakness and brokenness in turn awakens a humble and desperate cry for God in our hearts.

> The next step we can take in our
> pursuit of the knowledge of God is
> to seek Him in our daily lives.

Proverbs 2:3-5 promises, "For if you cry for discernment, lift your voice for understanding; if you seek her as silver and search for her as for hidden treasures; then you will discern the fear of the Lord and discover the knowledge of God." In other words, when we come before Him acknowledging our need, He releases His power and reveals Himself to us. Strength is not found in our own abilities, but in our dependence upon God. He resists the proud but gives grace to the humble (see James 4:6).

The next step we can take in our pursuit of the knowledge of God is to seek Him in our daily lives. Prayer, reading and studying the Scriptures, worship, and fellowship with other believers are all God-ordained paths leading to greater revelation. When we engage in these spiritual disciplines with humble, hungry hearts, God begins to remove every lie and demonic accusation that stands in opposition to the truth. It is important to realize this is a life-long process, not something we can check off of our spiritual to-do list. On this side of eternity we will always experience the resistance of the enemy in our pursuit of the knowledge of God. However, our pursuit is not in vain: "you will seek the Lord your God, and you will find Him if you search for Him with all your heart and all your soul" (Deut. 4:29).

NOTES

1. Loren Cunningham with Janice Rogers, *Making Jesus Lord: The Dynamic Power of Laying Down Your Rights*, (Seattle: YWAM Publishing, 1988), 134.

2. A.W. Tozer, *The Knowledge of the Holy*, (New York: HarperCollins Publishers, 1961), 1.

CHAPTER EIGHT

OUR ETERNAL IDENTITY

AFTER THE ENEMY LAUNCHES AN ATTACK AGAINST THE KNOWL-
edge of God in our lives, the next target is our identity. He
knows that when we experience a breakdown in the knowledge of God it leaves us vulnerable in the area of identity
and ultimately prevents us from fulfilling the two greatest
commandments.

> *"You shall love the Lord your God with all your
> heart, and with all your soul, and with all your
> mind." This is the great and foremost command-
> ment. The second is like it, "You shall love your
> neighbor as yourself"* (Matthew 22:37-39).

When I read these verses I cannot help but think, "That is
the problem: I *do* love my neighbor as I love myself!" Anyone
who has spent any length of time in the church is familiar with
the commandment to love others—and has probably heard

many times about all the ways they are failing in this department. Unfortunately, not many believers realize that their struggles to love others actually stem from identity wounds. We cannot give what we have not received; when we do not know how God loves us, we cannot love others in the same way.

This breakdown in the knowledge of God has produced an identity crisis in the lives of countless believers. How many of us have simply become accustomed to living with a constant chorus of self-doubt and criticism? "I will never overcome this issue. I'm not strong enough, I'm not gifted enough. God calls others to walk in power and victory—it isn't for me. I'm not worth it." We are inundated with these lies, and seldom do we challenge them or search the Scriptures to see what God actually says about who we are and what we mean to Him. This is exactly what the enemy wants! His goal is to prevent us from receiving revelation concerning our identity in Christ. When we are unaware of our great value and divine authority, we become vulnerable to deception and ineffective in advancing the kingdom.

The New Testament has a lot to say on the issue of identity. In fact, many of the apostles wrote about their responsibility to affirm the identity of believers for the purpose of strengthening the Body of Christ. These apostolic affirmations produced confidence, perseverance, and faith in the midst of demonic onslaught—and they are as relevant to us now as they were to the early church. There are three primary identities highlighted in the Pauline and Johannine epistles. The moment we accept Jesus Christ as our Savior, we become these three things:

1. Sons and daughters of God

2. The bride of Christ

3. Priests

> We cannot give what we have not
> received; when we do not know
> how God loves us, we cannot
> love others in the same way.

SONS AND DAUGHTERS

So also we, while we were children, were held in bondage under the elemental things of the world. But when the fullness of the time came, God sent forth His Son, born of a woman, born under the Law, so that He might redeem those who were under the Law, that we might receive the adoption as sons. Because you are sons, God has sent forth the Spirit of His Son into our hearts, crying, "Abba! Father!" **Therefore you are no longer a slave, but a son; and if a son, then an heir through God** *(Galatians 4:3-7).*

Paul wrote these words to a church struggling with legalism and the spirit of religion. He rebuked them for their lack of faith and then released this powerful reminder of their identity. They were children, not slaves, and they should live accordingly.

We find similar declarations in Ephesians and 1 John:

Just as He chose us in Him before the foundation of the world, that we would be holy and blameless before Him. In love **He predestined us to adoption as sons through Jesus Christ** *to Himself, according to the kind intention of His will (Ephesians 1:4-5).*

*See how great a love the Father has bestowed on us, that we would be called children of God; and such we are. For this reason the world does not know us, because it did not know Him. **Beloved, now we are children of God*** (1 John 3:1-2).

In fact, the New Testament is filled with references to our identity as children of God. You may be familiar with the verses, but have you ever stopped to ask why this point is so heavily emphasized? I stumbled across an answer to this very question when I began meditating on Romans 8. Actually, it is more accurate to say that God interrupted me with this chapter. I was sitting in the prayer room one day when I suddenly began to experience the powerful presence of the Holy Spirit. As I read through Romans 8, I was overwhelmed with the revelation of my identity as a son of God and my calling to take dominion over creation. I couldn't get over the fact that Jesus showed us what it means to be sons and daughters of God! When He walked on water, when He commanded the fig tree, when He restored blind eyes and deaf ears, He was operating out of His proper place as a son.

The more I immersed myself in the content of this chapter, the more I realized how central the revelation of our identity is to experiencing freedom from demonic strongholds and accusations. I want to walk through this chapter verse by verse and share some of the truths that have set my heart free. I also encourage you to set aside time to slowly, prayerfully read through the chapter and talk to God about it.

Therefore there is now no condemnation for those who are in Christ Jesus. For the law of the Spirit of life in Christ Jesus has set you free from the law of sin and of death (Romans 8:1-2).

Romans 8 is a beautiful dissertation on the power of our newfound standing as children of God. In the opening verses Paul highlights the connection between identity and freedom. Everyone who is in Christ has been liberated from the bondage of condemnation, sin, and death through the power of the Holy Spirit. This is not a theological point to master, but a supernatural truth to experience. The enemy no longer has jurisdiction over us! When we apply Jesus's death and resurrection to our lives, we receive the greatest deliverance of all—we are transferred from death to life, from guilt and shame to purity and holiness. This is the mission of the indwelling Holy Spirit. He came to set us free from the law of sin and death.

Sadly, many believers continue to live in bondage. The prison door has been opened but they stay in their cell, never experiencing the freedom given to them. Why is this? Why do so many continue to labor under condemnation? Paul answers this question when he writes about the importance of setting our minds on the things of the Spirit:

> *For those who are according to the flesh set their minds on the things of the flesh, but those who are according to the Spirit, the things of the Spirit. For the mind set on the flesh is death, but the mind set on the Spirit is life and peace, because the mind set on the flesh is hostile toward God; for it does not subject itself to the law of God, for it is not even able to do so, and those who are in the flesh cannot please God* (Romans 8:5-8).

Let's take a moment to break down these verses. According to Paul, our experience (life or death) is a product of our faith and confidence (the truths we agree with in our minds and hearts). When we activate our faith by focusing on the truths of the Spirit, we actually receive divine power to walk in those truths. The Holy Spirit transforms our minds and hearts, enabling us to live as citizens of another kingdom—as children of God rather than enemies. In other words, we walk out of our prison cells. Before, we just *knew* we were accepted by the Father, but now we *feel* accepted and it changes the way we live.

However, if we continue to see ourselves as citizens of this world we are actually putting our faith in the flesh. This makes us incredibly vulnerable to demonic attack. Remember our discussion of strongholds? Strongholds are fueled by our agreement with lies. If we focus on the lies of the enemy found in the fallen systems of this world, we will not have the power to walk in our true identity as sons and daughters. We may recognize the love of the Father as a theological truth, but we will not feel and experience it as a transforming reality. This is why we need to set our minds on the things of the Spirit and cultivate truth in our thoughts.

> *So then, brethren, we are under obligation, not to the flesh, to live according to the flesh—for if you are living according to the flesh, you must die; but if by the Spirit you are putting to death the deeds of the body, you will live. For **all who are being led by the Spirit of God, these are sons of God*** (Romans 8:12-14).

The opening of Romans 8 is devoted to the subject of the battle between the flesh and the Spirit. Paul exhorts us again and again to set our minds on things above and resist the flesh. However, in these verses he returns to the subject of identity.

Our ability to walk according to the Spirit is fundamentally related to our identity as sons of God. We will experience freedom from bondage and fear and receive power to resist the flesh when we embrace the truth of our eternal identity before the Father.

> He is our Abba—a tender, affectionate,
> and involved Dad who draws
> near and fills us with love.

For all who are being led by the Spirit of God, these are sons of God. For you have not received a spirit of slavery leading to fear again, but you have received a spirit of adoption as sons by which we cry out, "Abba! Father!" The Spirit Himself testifies with our spirit that we are children of God (Romans 8:14-16).

Paul specifically contrasts slavery and fear with adoption and sonship. Physically enslaved people fear the anger of their human masters, while spiritually enslaved people are tormented by fear of divine wrath. But the power of fear is broken through the revelation of adoption. I believe the body of Christ has only begun to scratch the surface of this reality. In essence, our spiritual adoption means this—complete acceptance.

Can you even imagine experiencing such a thing? When a couple decides to pursue adoption, they are given a choice. They are shown pictures and reports concerning a specific child, and then they decide whether or not they want it. If they do, they are choosing to completely love and accept a baby who has done absolutely nothing to win them over. They are making the statement, "I want this person and I commit to them, just the way they are, regardless of what happens." This is a picture of what God did for us. He looked at each of us and said, "I want this one. I choose to love and accept them forever. I will be their Father, and they will be My child."

In verse 15 Paul uses the word *Abba* to describe the cry of our hearts toward God. Jesus confronted the religious system of His day when He used this intimate, affectionate title to refer to the almighty Creator. God is our Father, yes, but not in the stern, distant, and patriarchal sense of the word. He is our Abba—a tender, affectionate, and involved Dad who draws near and fills us with love. In the same way a loving father has compassion on his child when they cry, or picks them up when they fall down, so our heavenly Father relates to us. His love is not altered by our weaknesses and failures; it is steadfast, compassionate, and unconditional. This truth is deeply offensive to those caught up in the spirit of religion and the desire to perform, but deeply liberating to those who are tired, weary, and at the end of their rope.

> *For I consider that the sufferings of this present time are not worthy to be compared with the glory that is to be revealed to us* (Romans 8:18).

Paul does not sugarcoat his message. Our eternal identity as sons and daughters of God comes at a price—when we carry the Spirit of God within, we will experience suffering through human persecution and demonic resistance. But this suffering ultimately unites us with Christ and bears witness to our heavenly adoption.

After addressing us individually regarding the battle between spirit and flesh, our divine adoption, and the expectation of suffering, Paul takes a step back and begins to address us corporately concerning an even greater issue. As sons and daughters of God, we have been handpicked to partner with Him in establishing His kingdom on earth and bringing redemption to all of creation. Our eternal identity is about more than personal breakthrough and provision—the earth is groaning and waiting for us to step into our divine mandate!

> *For the anxious longing of the creation waits eagerly for the revealing of the sons of God. For the creation was subjected to futility, not willingly, but because of Him who subjected it, in hope that the creation itself also will be set free from its slavery to corruption into the freedom of the glory of the children of God. For we know that the whole creation groans and suffers the pains of childbirth together until now. And not only this, but also we ourselves, having the first fruits of the Spirit, even we ourselves groan within ourselves, waiting eagerly for our adoption as sons, the redemption of our body* (Romans 8:19-23).

Creation was placed in a position of weakness at the fall. Not only did Adam and Eve lose their right to exercise dominion over the earth, but that right was usurped by Satan. He established demonic principalities and powers to govern the earth, and now creation suffers like a woman in labor as she longs and groans for relief and redemption. This redemption will only be released as we receive revelation of our identity. We are called to be coheirs with Christ and rulers over the created order. The spirit of adoption does more than free our hearts from rejection and teach us to cry "Abba"—it reveals our calling to exercise dominion and release the kingdom on the earth.

In essence, Paul is saying, "You have been liberated in Christ Jesus by the power of the Spirit. You are no longer subject to the law of sin and death. You are free and accepted. Now let this freedom release you into your eternal calling. Demonstrate the rule and reign of the kingdom on earth, and reveal the eternal purpose of God for all creation." This is our inheritance as the children of God, if we will only believe.

For many of us, this all sounds too good to be true. Paul is telling us to take our place, but we are struggling to believe God really loves us and wants us. We are easily offended, easily wounded, easily rejected—not great ruler material! Fortunately, the Holy Spirit knows us better than we know ourselves, and he inspired Paul to include powerful words of encouragement.

> *In the same way the Spirit also helps our weakness; for we do not know how to pray as we should, but the Spirit Himself intercedes for us with groanings too deep for words* (Romans 8:26).

This is so much bigger than a casual, "God loves you." Paul says just as creation is crying out, so God is crying out. The Holy Spirit prays for us and through us, partnering with creation in travail that we would know who we are. He *groans* and longs for the day when we will experience the fullness of redemption. Our ability to overcome is found in identifying with the truth of our weakness while at the same time trusting God and His ability to give us the power and comfort of the Holy Spirit. Through the Spirit we are affirmed in our sonship and granted the authority to partner with Him in intercession.

Ultimately these prayers will be fulfilled during the millennial reign of Christ. In that day the whole earth will be restored as the sons and daughters of God exercise dominion under the leadership of Jesus. But we live in the already/not yet kingdom. We have received the down payment of this fulfillment, the promised Holy Spirit. When Jesus walked the earth, He showed us what it meant to be a son or daughter of God. He walked on water. He took authority over the wind and waves and the fig trees. He healed broken bodies and raised the dead. And then He gave us the Spirit of adoption and told us to follow Him. That very same Spirit is now groaning and crying out until we wake up to who we are.

Paul is so caught up in the reality of all he is writing that the final verses seem to erupt from him in overwhelming faith and confidence. He is overpowered by the Holy Spirit as he sees the glorious end of the story. Creation has been subjected to futility, but Jesus is interceding for us. Furthermore, through His suffering and death He has made a way for us to be with Him forever. Though every principality and power of darkness wants to keep this truth hidden from the people of God, Paul boldly proclaims that nothing can prevent us from walking into our eternal identity and destiny:

> *What then shall we say to these things? If God is for us, who is against us? He who did not spare His own Son, but delivered Him over for us all, how will He not also with Him freely give us all things? Who will bring a charge against God's elect? God is the one who justifies; who is the one who condemns? Christ Jesus is He who died, yes, rather who was raised, who is at the right hand of God, who also intercedes for us. Who will separate us from the love of Christ? Will tribulation, or distress, or persecution, or*

famine, or nakedness, or peril, or sword? Just as it is written,

"For Your sake we are being put to death all day long; we were considered as sheep to be slaughtered."

But in all these things we overwhelmingly conquer through Him who loved us. *For I am convinced that neither death, nor life, nor angels, nor principalities, nor things present, nor things to come, nor powers, nor height, nor depth, nor any other created thing, will be able to separate us from the love of God, which is in Christ Jesus our Lord* (Romans 8:31-39).

Do we really understand who we are?

THE BRIDE OF CHRIST

We are not only sons and daughters; we are also the bride. In the Old Testament, and especially in the prophets, we find numerous references to Israel and Judah as a bride betrothed to God. This language portrays the depth of His commitment to His people and reflects the grief He felt when they were idolatrous and unfaithful.

*Now the word of the Lord came to me saying, "Go and proclaim in the ears of Jerusalem...I remember concerning you the devotion of your youth, **the love of your betrothals,** your following after Me in the wilderness, through a land not sown. Israel was holy to the Lord, the first of His harvest"* (Jeremiah 2:1-3).

> *And it shall be, in that day...that you will call Me "My Husband,"* and no longer call Me *"My Master"...I will betroth you to Me forever;* **yes, I will betroth you to Me** *in righteousness and justice, in lovingkindness and mercy; I will betroth you to Me in faithfulness, and you shall know the Lord* (Hosea 2:16, 19-20 NKJV).

In the New Testament, this language is picked up again in reference to the global body of believers. Not only is Israel the beloved bride; now every redeemed man, woman, and child enjoys that privileged and intimate relationship.

> *For this reason a man shall leave his father and mother and shall be joined to his wife, and the two shall become one flesh. This mystery is great; but I am speaking with reference to Christ and the church* (Ephesians 5:31-32).

> *Let us rejoice and be glad and give the glory to Him, for* **the marriage of the Lamb has come and His bride has made herself ready** (Revelation 19:7).

There are many dimensions to the bridal identity of believers, but I want to focus on two in particular. First, as the bride of Christ we are invited to walk in great intimacy with Him and to receive the affections of His heart. Second, our identity as His beloved creates the deepest confidence in us and strengthens our faith in the face of the enemy's accusations.

The Song of Solomon, perhaps more than any other book in the Bible, displays the intimacy and affection available to believers. Here we find a detailed portrait of the unfolding relationship between Solomon and his bride, the Shulamite maiden. Throughout church history there have been many interpretations of this book. While it is certainly a representation of the married love between a man and a woman, the book can also be understood as a divinely-inspired allegory depicting the progression of love and sanctification in a believer's life.

One of the primary themes we find emphasized in the Song of Solomon is that of God's desire for intimacy with us. This is reflected in Solomon's numerous calls for his bride to be near him and to join him in his work.

> *Rise up, my love, my fair one, and **come away!** O my dove, in the clefts of the rock, in the secret places of the cliff, **let me see your face, let me hear your voice**; for your voice is sweet, and your face is lovely* (Song of Solomon 2:13-14 NKJV).

In chapter 2 we hear a passionate plea for the bride to follow her bridegroom and "come away." Solomon longs to be with his beloved, even as Jesus longs for His bride, the Church, to be with Him: "Father, I desire that they also, whom You have given Me, be with Me where I am" (John 17:24).

Later in Song of Solomon, we see intimacy expressed through partnership. The Shulamite maiden wants to join her love in his vineyards, the place where he labors. This is another facet of intimacy. God not only desires to share the fullness of His heart with His people, but also to work with them in advancing the kingdom:

> *Come, my beloved, let us go out into the country, let us spend the night in the villages.* **Let us rise early and go to the vineyards;** *let us see whether the vine has budded and its blossoms have opened, and whether the pomegranates have bloomed. There I will give you my love* (Song of Solomon 7:11-12).

The reality of intimacy with God and the revelation of His heart and emotions toward us are the greatest gifts we receive when we walk into our bridal identity. However, being the bride of Christ is about more than freeing our hearts to receive God's love. It is also a strategic position from which we wage war against the enemy. This is powerfully demonstrated in the story of Esther. Her interactions with her husband, King Ahasuerus, reflect God's response to His bride when she approaches Him in humility and submission. Ultimately, we see that the heart of our King is moved and His power is released when we cry out for justice and salvation.

The story of Esther is one many of us are familiar with from our days in Sunday school. Hadassah, a young Jewish girl living in Susa, is selected to be the new bride of King Ahasuerus. She takes the name Esther and is established as queen in the palace, only to discover that Haman, a royal advisor, is plotting to annihilate her people. Esther, whose Jewish heritage was a secret, commits to fast and pray for three days. At the end of the three days, she risks everything by approaching the king without an invitation (an action which carries the death penalty) and begging for mercy.

Here is the king's response when Esther first enters the royal court uninvited:

> *When the king saw Esther the queen standing in the court,* **she obtained favor in his sight;** *and the king extended to Esther the golden scepter which was in his hand. So Esther came near and touched the top of the scepter. Then the king said to her, "What is troubling you, Queen Esther? And what is your request? Even to half of the kingdom it shall be given to you"* (Esther 5:2-3).

The phrase "she obtained favor in his sight" may seem cold and sterile, but it actually describes great emotion. Esther had just violated strict national protocol and her life hung in the balance. And what is the king's response? Not only does he stretch forth his scepter to save her, but he promises her up to half of his kingdom! He is completely overwhelmed with love. In the same way, when we approach God in humility and submission He is moved by us; He stretches forth the scepter of divine authority and releases His kingdom.

I have a private study in my home, and when I am using it absolutely no one is allowed to enter and bother me. It is my escape, the place where I go to read, pray, and research. However, if my wife opens the door you better believe that I will let her in! She is the only person who can interrupt me. When I see her, she doesn't have to ask my permission to enter or wait till I am done. She has access because I am completely in love with her. This is our position with God! We need to perceive ourselves as His highly favored bride. We have access to His presence, His affections, and His emotions. We can interrupt Him any time.

Esther benefitted from more than King Ahasuerus's favor. She also benefited from his wrath.

> *Esther said, "A foe and an enemy is this wicked Haman!"* **Then Haman became terrified before the king and queen.** *The king arose in his anger from drinking wine and went into the palace garden; but Haman stayed to beg for his life from Queen Esther, for he saw that harm had been determined against him by the king. Now when the king returned from the palace garden into the place where they were drinking wine, Haman was falling on the couch where Esther was. Then the king said, "Will he even assault the queen with me in the house?" ...* **So they hanged Haman on the gallows which he had prepared for Mordecai, and the king's anger subsided** (Esther 7:6-8, 10).

> No true husband will stand by while someone threatens his wife.

No true husband will stand by while someone threatens his wife. Like the king in the book of Esther, our God will take a stand for His beloved and silence her enemies. We must cling to this truth when we are interceding for breakthrough: God's favor rests upon us and He will rise up to defeat every demonic power that threatens us. But we must have the faith and patience to wait for God's justice and not give in to the temptation to take matters into our own hands.

The second dimension of our bridal identity I want to highlight is the confidence and trust that the revelation of God's love engenders within us. When we see ourselves as God's beloved, we are motivated to run into His presence with total abandonment and to trust in His goodness even if we have fallen and failed. In times of weakness, we need to remember that God loved us from before the beginning of time and His love is unchanging. He knew all our faults, He saw every area of brokenness and sin, yet He still chose to create us and love us. This knowledge is the foundation of our security.

> God is committed to show us everlasting mercy, not because of anything we have done or will do, but because of His burning desire to be with us!

It is also one of the most contested truths in the lives of individual believers. How many of us regularly battle feelings of shame, guilt, rejection, and fear when we stumble in sin? Instead of running to God for forgiveness and comfort, we run from Him and end up prolonging the cycles of failure and brokenness. We need to arm ourselves with the revelation of our bridal identity and God's commitment to us in order to push the enemy out of the way and align ourselves with truth. A wife will not be vulnerable with her husband unless she knows he is completely committed to the relationship. In the same way, we will experience breakthrough in our ability to draw near to God in moments of weakness as we discover His deep and abiding love for us.

It is incredibly important to realize that this love and commitment is not based on our performance or merit. It is based on the new covenant—the finished work of the cross—and our faith in that covenant. In other words, God is committed to show us everlasting mercy, not because of anything we have done or will do, but because of His burning desire to be with us! The author of Hebrews spends many chapters explaining the significance of this new covenant. Again and again he emphasizes that the covenant we receive in Jesus Christ is new, greater, and eternal.

> *Jesus has become the **guarantee of a better covenant*** (Hebrews 7:22).

> *He is also the mediator of a better covenant, which has been **enacted on better promises*** (Hebrews 8:6).

> *Now the God of peace, who brought up from the dead the great Shepherd of the sheep through **the blood of the eternal covenant**, even Jesus our Lord, equip you in every good thing to do His will* (Hebrews 13:20-21).

Jesus told the crowds in Galilee that they could not enter the kingdom of God unless their righteousness exceeded that of the scribes and Pharisees (see Matt. 5:20). Have you ever wondered what He really meant? He was purposefully calling the people to a standard they could not attain! But in doing so, He exposed their inability to earn their salvation. The only way into the kingdom of God is through faith in Christ's sacrifice and forgiveness. This is why it is a new and better covenant; it is based on a perfect Man and His ability to fulfill the law and prophets, atone for the sins of humanity, and reconcile men and women with God. It has nothing to do with our own abilities or righteousness.

And this covenant is eternal. Our failures and brokenness do not nullify its promises. Just as a man and woman covenant before God to love one another for better or worse and to remain faithful no matter what may happen, so our heavenly Bridegroom has established a covenant with us that stands even when we stumble and fall. He has already paid the price and made a way for us. All He asks in return is that we believe in all He has accomplished and remain in His love.

PRIESTS BEFORE GOD

To Him who loves us and released us from our sins by His blood—and He has made us to be a kingdom, priests to His God and Father—to Him be the glory and the dominion forever and ever (Revelation 1:5-6).

One of the most neglected and marginalized truths concerning the identity of believers is that in Christ every man, woman, and child is called to be a priest. When we hear the word *priest*, many of us probably picture a Catholic cleric in his vestments. Perhaps we imagine a scene straight out of the Old Testament—the Levite in his linen robes and ephod, preparing to sacrifice an animal on the altar. What we often fail to realize is that the New Testament contains many references to the priesthood of believers. This is not an outdated job title. It is an eternal calling, and one that is central to our spiritual identity.

You see, being a priest is not about robes and ceremonies. Fundamentally, it is about encountering and experiencing God. This has been His desire from the very beginning. When God called Abram and promised to make him into a mighty nation, He was cultivating a people who would belong to Him alone and enter His presence. When He spoke to Moses on Mount Sinai, this was the first message He passed on to the nation of Israel:

> *Now then, if you will indeed obey My voice and keep My covenant, then you shall be My own possession among all the peoples, for all the earth is Mine; and **you shall be to Me a kingdom of priests** and a holy nation* (Exodus 19:5-6).

This was more than a job description; it was an identity. Israel was called to be a nation where the people were defined by their priesthood. Worship, prayer, sacrifice, and the presence of God were meant to be their primary signifiers. In addition, this calling was integral to the establishment of God's kingdom. The passage specifically refers to the people as a *kingdom* of priests. In other words, their ministry to God was the key to releasing His divine government on earth. Notice that the entire nation is included in this divine invitation. God did not just call Aaron and the tribe of Levi—he called all of Israel.

In Leviticus 9 we are given a picture of this calling. Aaron and his sons had just completed seven days of consecration, and now they were prepared to offer sacrifices and encounter God:

> *Then Aaron lifted up his hands toward the people and blessed them, and he stepped down after making the sin offering and the burnt offering and the peace offerings. Moses and Aaron went into the tent of meeting. When they came out and blessed the people, the glory of the Lord*

appeared to all the people. Then fire came out from before the Lord and consumed the burnt offering and the portions of fat on the altar; and when all the people saw it, they shouted and fell on their faces (Leviticus 9:22-24).

I sometimes think we are so distracted by the unfamiliar rituals and ceremonies found in passages like this that we miss the profound simplicity of the encounters they describe. Moses and Aaron entered into the holy place and met with God. Then they stretched out their hands to bless the people of Israel and the Spirit of God appeared as fire, consuming the offering on the altar and causing every single person to fall on their face in repentance and worship. Can you picture the waves of glory that must have emanated from Moses and Aaron in that moment?

> We are made to encounter God and then go out into the world, stretch out our hands, and release revelation and power.

This is what we are made to do! We are made to encounter God and then go out into the world, stretch out our hands, and release revelation and power. The priestly calling is not just for the Levites and the Israelites anymore; it is also for every participant in the New Covenant. Look at what the writer of Hebrews has to say about our access to God:

Therefore, brethren, since we have confidence to enter the holy place by the blood of Jesus, by a new and living way which He inaugurated for us through the veil, that is, His flesh (Hebrews 10:19-20).

We are no longer required to sacrifice animals because we are covered by the blood of Jesus. We are no longer removed from the holy of holies because His wounds have forever torn the veil of separation. Like Israel, we are called to draw near to God, but we respond to this calling in a different way—a new and living way.

> *And since we have a great priest over the house of God* (Hebrews 10:21)

Jesus is more than just our great high priest. When the writer of Hebrews declares "we have a great priest over the house of God," he is making a statement about the divine method of government. Jesus rules and reigns from heaven as a king-priest. The prophet Zechariah goes so far as to call Him "a priest on his throne" (Zech. 6:13). Not only does Jesus intercede for us in the courts of heaven, but He also releases His power on our behalf as a mighty king.

> *Let us draw near with a sincere heart in full assurance of faith, having our hearts sprinkled clean from an evil conscience and our bodies washed with pure water* (Hebrews 10:22).

Holy place, through the veil, sprinkling, washing—these are all references to the Old Testament ministry of the priests. In Leviticus 8 we find a detailed description of the rituals Moses and Aaron had to perform before they could enter the tent of meeting. It was a seven-day process involving multiple sacrifices, washing with water, anointing with oil, and sprinkling with blood. If any of the steps were skipped or performed inadequately, the price was death. In light of this reality, how astonishing is it that we have immediate and unhindered access to God? We do not have to stand outside the tent of meeting for seven days to purify ourselves; we can simply enter in as priests under the New Covenant and experience His glory with confidence and boldness.

Peter echoes the author of Hebrews when he describes the calling and identity of believers:

> *You also, as living stones, are being built up as a spiritual house for* **a holy priesthood,** *to offer up spiritual sacrifices acceptable to God through Jesus Christ* (1 Peter 2:5).

> *But you are a chosen race,* **a royal priesthood,** *a holy nation, a people for God's own possession, so that you may proclaim the excellencies of Him who has called you out of darkness into His marvelous light* (1 Peter 2:9).

Unfortunately, the concept of being a people called solely to minister to God is not a familiar one for many believers today. If we are honest, many of us think that God needs us to go out and do more—more evangelizing, more giving, more volunteering, more teaching and preaching. While we are supposed to do these things, we will find ourselves burnt out and disconnected from a deeper sense of purpose if we do them first. Moses and Aaron stretched out their hands to the people *after* they entered into the presence of God. They understood that before they could lead the people of Israel, they had to be what they were called to be—priests created to worship God and encounter His glory.

Do you realize what this means? You are already defined. Your identity is secure and nothing can stop you from fulfilling your highest calling. It doesn't matter if you are a student, a secretary, a pastor, a missionary, a businessperson or a stay-at-home parent, because you are first and foremost a priest. You don't have to jockey for position in the kingdom and you don't have to buy in to the world's systems that define people based on their title or position. When you walk into your prayer closet you are engaging in the highest calling available to you. You are operating in your eternal identity and function as a priest.

> The power and rule of the kingdom
> are released through prayer.

This identity not only establishes our proximity to God, but also establishes our authority. We have already seen the relationship between priesthood and government in several of the verses examined earlier: Jesus is the king-priest who rules and reigns through His priestly ministry (see Heb. 10:21; Zech. 6:13), and believers are called to be a kingdom of priests (see Rev. 1:5-6). These verses—and many others we will not take the time to examine here—serve to illustrate the amazing fact that the power and rule of the kingdom are released through prayer. Look at the language used in Revelation 5:10 when the saints and angels worship Jesus as the destiny of every believer is revealed: "You have made them to be a kingdom and priests to our God; and they will reign upon the earth." We are priests, and therefore we will reign.

In the next chapter, I want to look at the subject of governmental intercession. While all believers operate individually in their priestly calling, there is a corporate dimension to this ministry as well. Nothing shatters the kingdom of darkness like a unified, praying Church!

CHAPTER NINE

GOVERNMENTAL INTERCESSION

I AM JUST GOING TO SAY IT: THERE ARE A LOT OF UNHEALTHY, unbiblical ways to confront principalities. Many ministries claim they have the formula, the solution, the five easy steps to reclaim territory from the enemy, yet very little fruit materializes from their efforts. While I believe there is value in identifying and understanding the strongholds governing a particular geographic area (a practice commonly referred to as spiritual mapping), I do not believe that a group of intercessors should show up, confront the power of a regional demonic stronghold through targeted prayer, and then pack their bags and leave. The transformation achieved through this method is rarely sustainable, and can be a waste of energy and resources.

(I am not referring here to gatherings where believers intercede for regional restoration and revival and ask God to break the power of the enemy. I fully support such gatherings, and have participated in many solemn assemblies led by ministries like The Call. It is powerful when the people of God come together to fast, pray, and seek His face. Instead, I am referring to the practice of traveling to the high places in a nation like Thailand and commanding the demons of false religion to leave, knowing that thousands of Buddhist monks will simply invite the demons back.)

Then there are the believers who think it is their job to "take the fight to the enemy." If they can minister effectively to individuals and see them set free from demonic oppression, why not up the ante and kick the local principality or power out of the region? While it is true that believers possess great authority in the kingdom of God, the testimony of the Scriptures reveals that not everyone has the power to individually confront high-ranking demonic beings. Remember the words of warning given to Job concerning his ability to overcome the enemy? "Lay your hand on [Satan]; remember the battle; you will not do it again!" (Job 41:8). This warning is not meant to promote fear, but rather encourage wisdom. If an individual feels led to personally confront a principality, they should have a very clear word from the Lord regarding how to proceed. Jehu received a specific anointing to deal with Jezebel, but he is the exception. I do not think many believers are given such assignments.

I learned this lesson the hard way during my season of ministry in France. After I graduated from the Brownsville Revival School I traveled to Paris for a three-month internship. While there I immersed myself in deliverance ministry and consequently was exposed to the very real forces of darkness operating in that city. I have never encountered more witchcraft in my life! Even the churches filled with life and the power of the Spirit were plagued by curses and black magic.

As a young man who had spent the previous few years in the midst of a revival, I was very zealous when it came to spiritual warfare. My attitude can be best described as "bring it on!" I was willing to go anywhere and take on any demonic power. After witnessing the overwhelming spiritual oppression in Paris, I had a brilliant idea. I decided to anoint the entire city with oil. So I gathered a group of friends, bought a bunch of squirt guns and filled them with oil, rented roller blades, and took off. We probably covered twenty miles in one day. We started at Notre Dame and hit every major landmark (the Arc de Triomphe, the Louvre, Napoleon's tomb, etc.). North, south, east, west—I was squirting everything and rebuking principalities like crazy. At the end of the day I was looking toward the Palais Garnier and watching the sun set when suddenly a large red scroll unrolled in front of the building. The scroll was so large that it was clearly visible to me although I was several miles away. And pictured on this red scroll was Jesus hanging on the cross. As I observed this remarkable sight, I heard the Holy Spirit say, "I have a remnant in this city, and I am going to send a revival. The floods in the natural will confirm the floods of revival I will send to this city."

> Not everyone has the power to individually confront high-ranking demonic beings.

Two years later, Paris experienced some of the worst flooding in its history. I believe this was confirmation of the word the Lord spoke to me on that day. However, it is a miracle that I lived to see this confirmation. The morning after I anointed Paris I woke up with a severe fever and dysentery. For several days my temperature remained at 106 degrees, and I almost died. I am convinced that the prayers of the nearly two thousand students back at the Brownsville Revival School are the only reason I recovered. This is what happens when you go out and pick a fight with principalities![1] Since that experience my approach to corporate spiritual warfare has dramatically shifted.

PRINCIPALITIES AND POWERS

Dangerous mistakes are made when men and women do not understand their enemy. Even Elijah, one of the most powerful prophets in the Old Testament, ran for his life after he confronted the power of Baal on Mount Carmel (see 1 Kings 18:17–19:3). His confrontation was successful, but in the aftermath he ended up hiding in a cave and begging God to end his life! If we want to avoid similar miscalculations, we need to begin by looking at what the Bible has to say about the nature and function of principalities and powers.

In an earlier chapter we discussed the anatomy of demonic strongholds. Demons exploit the vulnerabilities of the human soul in order to get us to buy in to lies and agree with darkness. Once we are in agreement, they have the authority to oppress and manipulate us. These same dynamics apply to corporate spiritual warfare. Just as low-ranking demons are assigned by Satan to attack and harass individuals, so high-ranking demons are assigned to attack and control entire people groups and geographic regions. The Bible refers to these demons as "principalities and powers."

The book of Daniel gives us the clearest picture of this demonic hierarchy. In his old age, Daniel is visited by an angelic messenger during a season of prayer and fasting. The angel tells Daniel that his appearance was delayed due to demonic warfare:

> *But the prince of the kingdom of Persia was withstanding me for twenty-one days; then behold,*

> *Michael, one of the chief princes, came to help me, for I had been left there with the kings of Persia* (Daniel 10:13).

There are two beings specifically named in this passage. Michael is described as a chief prince and is clearly an angelic being sent to aid the messenger. In fact, two other scriptures reference a powerful angelic being named Michael. In the book of Jude he is given the title "archangel," and in Revelation he is described as the captain of an army of angels (see Jude 1:9; Rev. 12:7). This suggests that he possesses great rank and authority in the kingdom of God.

The second being is simply given a title: "the prince of the kingdom of Persia." There are several things we can infer based on the details of the passage. First, because he is resisting the messengers of God, the prince of Persia must be a demonic being. Second, as he is given the same title as Michael (they are both called "prince"), his rank and authority in the kingdom of darkness must be equivalent. If Michael is the leader of a company of angelic warriors, then it seems likely the prince of Persia also has numerous demonic spirits under his command. Third, based on the fact that the angelic messenger was forced to call for reinforcements in his battle, we can infer that the prince of Persia is very strong—strong enough to overwhelm lesser spirits and temporarily prevent the plans of God. Finally, because *Persia* is incorporated into his title, we can infer that his authority in the kingdom of darkness is associated with a particular nation and/or geographic region.

What does any of this have to do with us? The answer is that the book of Daniel lifts the veil between the natural and spiritual realm and gives us a glimpse of what is really going on all around us. Demonic beings with authority over nations and regions still exist today. Not only do they exist, but they dramatically affect our lives and play a significant role in shaping the course of human history.

DO NOT BE IGNORANT

Now that we have examined the nature of principalities from a biblical standpoint, it is time for us to look at what the Scriptures have to say about confronting and overcoming these demonic beings. I believe the majority of believers are dangerously ignorant when it comes to warfare with principalities. Paul addresses this subject more directly than any other author in the New Testament—and interestingly enough, his writings include a specific warning to believers: "Do not be ignorant."

This exhortation actually occurs several times in Paul's letters. In each instance he is writing to believers who are in danger of being deceived by the enemy. Stop for a moment and consider the following list:

1. Do not be ignorant concerning the resurrection of the dead (1 Thess. 4:13).

2. Do not be ignorant concerning idolatry (1 Cor. 10:1).

3. Do not be ignorant concerning spiritual gifts (1 Cor. 12:1).

4. Do not be ignorant concerning Israel (Rom. 11:25).

Imagine that someone asked you to create a list of subjects that are essential for all Christians to know and understand. What would your list look like? I am guessing that the four subjects highlighted above would barely make it onto most of our lists! Yet these were subjects Paul cared about passionately and wanted to defend against demonic deception and error.

It is not my intention to closely examine all four here. (For more information on spiritual gifts and the power of the Holy Spirit, you can refer back to chapter three.) Instead I want to highlight the importance of understanding God's plans for Israel and the mystery of one new man. You see, Paul actually tells us what will make demonic principalities and powers sit up and take note of the Church. One of the few times that he references principalities in his letters, it is in the context of discussing God's redemptive plans for Jew and Gentile.

> *How that by revelation He made known to me the mystery...which in other ages was not made known to the sons of men, as it has now been revealed by the Spirit to His holy apostles and prophets* (Ephesians 3:3, 5 NKJV).

One of the few times that Paul references principalities in his letters, it is in the context of discussing God's redemptive plans for Jew and Gentile.

As an apostle, the grace and anointing of the Holy Spirit enabled Paul to make the mysteries of God known. He was divinely commissioned to communicate not just the identity of Jesus Christ and the saving news of the gospel, but also the identity of the Church—an identity formerly shrouded in mystery but now revealed to all.

*That the Gentiles should be fellow heirs, of the
same body, and partakers of His promise in Christ
through the gospel* (Ephesians 3:6 NKJV).

Paul's letter to the Ephesians contains some of the most
foundational teachings on the identity, purpose, and function
of the Church in the New Testament—and this verse lies at the
heart of it all. It is astonishing to realize that one of the primary
mandates of his apostleship was the proclamation of Jew and
Gentile as fellow heirs. Paul saw this truth as an integral and
significant element of his teaching on the Church's identity.

*To me, who am less than the least of all the saints,
this grace was given, that I should preach among
the Gentiles the unsearchable riches of Christ,
and to make all see what is the fellowship of the
mystery, which from the beginning of the ages
has been hidden in God who created all things
through Jesus Christ; to the intent that now **the
manifold wisdom of God might be made
known by the church to the principalities
and powers in the heavenly places**, according
to the eternal purpose which He accomplished in
Christ Jesus our Lord* (Ephesians 3:8-11 NKJV).

Suddenly, in the midst of a discussion of Jew and Gentile,
Paul declared that this truth is meant to be displayed before
principalities and powers. There is really only one other verse
that directly addresses the subject of believers confronting principalities (see Eph. 6:12). In other words, the mystery of Jew
and Gentile becoming one new man in Christ is an important
component of corporate spiritual warfare. When the Church
is disconnected from its identity and eternal purpose, it is no

threat to the powers of darkness. The display of God's wisdom concerning the nation of Israel is the primary scriptural way to confront demonic principalities. I believe we have drifted from the original apostolic foundations of the Church as outlined in the book of Ephesians. Is it possible that the enemy is unmoved by our denominational structures and systems because we are not walking in our eternal purpose? Does the Church today actually operate under the influence of darkness in this arena? If so, we need to reclaim our purpose and authority by returning to the apostolic and prophetic foundations of our faith.

> The mystery of Jew and Gentile becoming one new man in Christ is an important component of corporate spiritual warfare.

In order to understand the connection between God's redemptive plan for Israel and spiritual warfare in the everyday lives of believers, we need to examine Israel's calling. When God first visited Abraham and told him to leave his father's house, several significant promises were made concerning Abraham's destiny. God declared He would make Abraham into a great nation and that through his descendants *all families of the earth would be blessed* (see Gen. 12:2-3). When we read this promise, most of us assume it refers to the Messiah who came from Abraham's line. This was certainly a key component of God's covenant with Abraham, but there is more to it. The children of Israel were chosen to display the nature and character of God. The fact that His presence resided in their midst distinguished them from every other nation. As a kingdom of priests, they were uniquely called to be a light to the peoples of the earth.

However, from the beginning of human history the enemy has sought to prevent men and women from manifesting the glory of God. When he succeeded in hardening the hearts of the children of Israel—leading them into rebellion and ultimately causing them to reject their Messiah—it appeared as though the testimony of God had been extinguished. But this was not the case.

> ***God has not rejected His people whom He foreknew.*** *...I say then, they did not stumble so as to fall, did they? May it never be!* ***But by their transgression salvation has come to the Gentiles****, to make them jealous. Now if their transgression is riches for the world and their failure is riches for the Gentiles, how much more will their fulfillment be!* (Romans 11:2, 11-12)

In his letter to the Roman church, Paul describes the heart of his mission to the Gentile world. He declares he was commissioned by the Holy Spirit to raise up Gentile believers as fellow heirs of salvation with Israel in order to provoke the Jews to jealousy. As Gentile believers, we have received the Holy Spirit. We now carry the presence of God and our lives embody His testimony. Formerly the covenants and promises were for the Jews alone, but in Christ the dividing wall between Jew and Gentile has been demolished.

This does not mean Gentile believers have replaced Israel in the plans of God, however.

> *For I do not desire, brethren, that you should be ignorant of this mystery, lest you should be wise in your own opinion, that blindness in part*

has happened to Israel until the fullness of the
Gentiles has come in (Romans 11:25 NKJV).

Paul specifically states that Gentiles should not be ignorant or arrogant concerning the eternal purposes of God for
Israel. We have not replaced the Jews. Rather, Gentile believers
are called to make the Jews "jealous." What does this mean?
It means that when our lives manifest the blessings of God—
blessings originally promised to the Jews—they are provoked.
It awakens their hunger for the spiritual inheritance promised
to their forefathers, and it turns their hearts back to God. Ultimately, the Father desires that all Israel would be saved through
the witness and testimony of Gentile believers.

This is our calling and inheritance, and we will not experience the full measure of all God has for us until we are walking
in the reality of the one new man. Yet how many of us grew up
in a congregation where we were taught about our identity as
a corporate witness to the Jewish people? When you were first
saved, did anyone tell you about your calling to provoke the
Jews to jealousy and to identify with their suffering by bearing
the reproach of Christ? For most of us, the answer to these questions is "no." We are in a corporate identity crisis. The enemy's
assault has disconnected us from the revelation that salvation is
first for the Jew (see Rom. 1:16). In fact, many believers are told
the Gentiles have now replaced Israel in the redemptive plans
of God. This deception is a demonic attack against the eternal
purpose of the Church. Our enemy does not want us to know
who we truly are and what we are called to be.

When Paul wrote about the revelation of the mystery of
Christ, he understood that this revelation was the founda-
tion that would enable the Church to overcome principalities.
That is why he declared that the manifold wisdom of God

would be made known *to every spiritual power* by the church (see Eph. 3:10). When we overcome demonic deception and begin to labor for the salvation of the Jews, our very lifestyle displays the wisdom of God to principalities and destroys the enemy's strongholds.

CONFRONTING PRINCIPALITIES AND POWERS AS THE CHURCH

I am convinced that believers operating in unity can see the forces of darkness expelled from their region. This conviction is based not only on Paul's exhortation regarding the identity of the Church, but also on several scriptures which illustrate kingdom methods of warfare. In the Bible we see that God promises to release His power over entire geographic regions when His people come to Him in humble repentance and intercession. In fact, I believe that the corporate worship and intercession of the Church is one of the most effective weapons to defeat the enemy and take back areas of society previously under the jurisdiction of demonic principalities.

> When we pray concerning demonic principalities we should address God and ask Him to move on our behalf and push back darkness.

Before we examine a few specific scriptures that illustrate this point, let me make one thing clear: when I refer to corporate worship and intercession, I do not mean that groups of believers should directly rebuke demonic powers. Most of the time when this happens, men and women are actually overstepping their spiritual authority and opening themselves up to demonic backlash. When we pray concerning demonic princi-palities, we should address God and ask Him to move on our behalf and push back darkness. This is the most effective way to pray against forces of darkness. Rather than confronting the enemy directly, we simply petition the Trinity to deal with the strongholds in a particular region. Here is an example: "Father, in the name of Jesus I/we ask You to push back the forces of darkness in our land. Establish Your truth and send Your pres-ence. Release deliverance and the spirit of revelation regarding Your will." Notice that the emphasis is on praying directly to God, not rebuking Satan. However, it would be a mistake to think that praying in this correct manner is the only necessary component of our warfare. It is not enough to pray against the enemy; we must allow our worship and intercession to trans-form us until our very lives confront darkness.

The reality of God's kingdom living within men and women is one of the greatest threats to the enemy. You see, prin-cipalities and powers are not disturbed by church gatherings. They are disturbed by the power of the Spirit. A congrega-tion may hand out tracts, hold Sunday morning services and Wednesday evening Bible studies, and even tithe regularly with-out attracting much of the enemy's attention. What matters is whether or not the members of the congregation are walking in the authority and power of God. When believers are living lives of holiness, operating in the spirit of truth with humility, and working together in unity, they don't need to march around proclaiming that Jesus is Lord over their city.

> The reality of God's kingdom living
> within men and women is one of the
> greatest threats to the enemy.

I have become convinced of this truth after many years of experience, but anyone studying the subject of corporate spiritual warfare for the first time must wrestle with the fact that the Bible has very little to say about overcoming principalities. Instead, it gives us numerous teachings on how to draw near to God. These two topics may seem unrelated, but I believe there is a very close and strategic connection between them. James promises us that if we draw near to God, He will draw near to us (see James 4:8). Can you think of a greater weapon against darkness than the presence of God?

One of the passages that illustrates the power of God's presence is found in 2 Chronicles:

> *If My people who are called by My name will humble themselves, and pray and seek My face, and turn from their wicked ways, then I will hear from heaven, and will forgive their sin and heal their land* (2 Chronicles 7:14 NKJV).

After Solomon completed the temple, God appeared to him and made this declaration. It was a prescription for national, corporate breakthrough. When Israel experienced divine judgment, the solution was simple—repent from the heart, turn to God with prayer and fasting, and He will heal the land. Notice that God did not say, "if My people will rebuke demonic principalities and powers, then I will heal their land." He said, "humble yourselves, pray, and turn from your sins." In context, this passage addresses the subject of divine judgment, not demonic assault. However, the same principles may be effectively applied to spiritual warfare. When the people of God seek His face together in humility and repentance, it releases revival and transformation.

King Hezekiah followed this prescription and led the nation of Judah in corporate repentance. The results were nothing short of miraculous.

> *Hezekiah became king when he was twenty-five years old; and he reigned twenty-nine years in Jerusalem. And his mother's name was Abijah, the daughter of Zechariah. He did right in the sight of the Lord, according to all that his father David had done. In the first year of his reign, in the first month,* **he opened the doors of the house of the Lord and repaired them** (2 Chronicles 29:1-3).

Before we look at these specific verses, let's examine the context. Hezekiah's predecessor, Ahaz, was a wicked king. He practiced idolatry and child sacrifice, and the people of Judah followed him. This led to military defeat and the loss of 120,000 lives. When Hezekiah assumed the throne he was faced with a ruined temple, a demoralized population, and entrenched demonic strongholds fueled by occult practices. So what did he do? The Scripture says that he began repairing the temple in the first month of the first year of his reign. In other words, restoring prayer and worship in the land was his number one priority! He understood the importance of providing a place where the people could encounter their God. And Hezekiah did not stop there.

> *Then he said to them, "Listen to me, O Levites. Consecrate yourselves now, and consecrate the house of the Lord, the God of your fathers, and carry the uncleanness out from the holy place. ...My sons, do not be negligent now,* **for the**

Lord has chosen you to stand before Him, *to minister to Him, and to be His ministers* *and burn incense* (2 Chronicles 29:5, 11).

He called the priests back to their identity because he was convinced that prayer and worship would open the heavens over the land and prepare the hearts of the people to return to God.

While the whole assembly worshiped, the singers *also sang and the trumpets sounded; all this contin-* *ued until the burnt offering was finished. Now at* *the completion of the burnt offerings,* ***the king*** ***and all who were present with him bowed*** ***down and worshiped****. Moreover, King Hezekiah* *and the officials ordered the Levites to sing praises* *to the Lord with the words of David and Asaph* *the seer. So they sang praises with joy, and bowed* *down and worshiped* (2 Chronicles 29:28-30).

The effects of these reforms were dramatic. When the regional superpower, Assyria, threatened Judah and besieged Jerusalem, God intervened on behalf of His people. An angel entered the enemy camp and struck down 185,000 Assyrians in a single night. Those who survived swiftly retreated, leaving Jerusalem untouched (see Isa. 37). This was a dramatic fulfill-ment of the promise God made to Solomon: "if the nation prays and turns from their sin, I will heal their land." The nation of Judah won a significant victory in the natural and spiritual realms without ever directly confronting the enemy. They won with prayer and worship.

The same methods of warfare are available to the Church today. When we gather with other believers to seek God through intercession, adoration, and repentance, together we become a resting place for His presence. This is why I am convinced that continual prayer and worship is necessary to establish and maintain freedom from strongholds in geographic regions. Only the presence of God can release revival, transformation, and corporate spiritual breakthrough.

COMMUNITY

So far I have emphasized the importance of corporate prayer and worship in driving out strongholds of darkness. However, 2 Chronicles 7:14 also highlights the need for humility and repentance. God isn't looking for "quick fix" prayer meetings— meetings where people in crisis show up to pray without ever changing their way of life. He is looking for transformed hearts and consecrated lives. This is yet another reason why spiritual warfare is most effective in the context of community.

The apostle John wrote that if we have fellowship with one another, the blood of Jesus cleanses us from all unrighteousness (see 1 John 1:7). I believe one of the ways this happens is through the exposure of our personal sin and brokenness. I often tell my students that I used to think I was holy until I got married. After my wedding, however, I found out I wasn't really very holy. I was just used to getting my own way! Once I had to live in community with someone, practicing humility and finding ways to compromise, I quickly discovered many personal blind spots. This is one of the numerous reasons why the body of Christ needs one another.

We will never fulfill the command to walk in righteousness outside of the context of godly community. Fellowship with other believers strengthens, sharpens, reveals, and encourages us. John did not just state that fellowship with other believers releases cleansing; he declared it was a direct result of our ability to walk in the light:

> *God is Light, and in Him there is no darkness at all...if we walk in the Light as He Himself is in the Light, we have fellowship with one another, and the blood of Jesus His Son cleanses us from all sin* (1 John 1:5, 7).

Our relationships are the litmus test of our spirituality. This is why in His very first sermon Jesus spent so much time talking about how we treat others. In fact, He directly tied our inheritance of the kingdom to our treatment of those around us. Do you want to walk in the authority of God? Then you need to be meek and gentle, you need to forgive as you have been forgiven, and you need to love your enemies (see Matt. 5). In the kingdom, power and character go hand in hand.

> Our relationships are the litmus
> test of our spirituality.

It is so easy to forget this in the middle of spiritual warfare! We become easily overwhelmed with the external forces of darkness resisting us, and we forget the equally-important battle on the inside for clean hands and a pure heart. But if we will give our all to winning the hidden battle for righteousness, God promises to fight the bigger battles for us.

> *If My people who are called by My name will humble themselves, and pray and seek My face, and turn from their wicked ways, then I will*

hear from heaven, and will forgive their sin and heal their land. I long to draw close to those who worship Me. I long to call them into relationship and empower them to walk in My ways. No principality or power can resist the Church when she steps into her true identity (2 Chronicles 7:14, paraphrased and expanded).

NOTE

1. For more information on this subject, I highly recommend John Paul Jackson's book *Needless Casualties of War.*

A NOTE ON TIMES AND SEASONS

OVER THE YEARS I HAVE HAD THE OPPORTUNITY TO MINISTER to many people at different stages in their walk with God. Often the differences are apparent as soon as I begin praying: some individuals experience the power of God in a tangible way, while others struggle to sense His presence. This struggle may be caused by demonic interference, or it may simply be part of the spiritual season known as the wilderness.

We have spent much of this book discussing the schemes of the enemy, but it is important to remember that not everything is demonic. God sometimes allows us to experience difficult, dry seasons in order to test and mature our faith. I remember very clearly when I first encountered this reality in my own life. The months of ministry in Paris were an amazing time for me. Although I was confronted with intense spiritual warfare, I also saw the power of God released in dramatic, tangible ways. I knew I had experienced the glory of my calling, and so my expectations for the future were sky high when I left France and returned to Pensacola, Florida to get married. However, shortly after my arrival in the States, the Brownsville Revival ended. There was a split in the church, and the pain and turmoil this caused in my own life and the lives of many others was significant. Every last bit of stability in my life and ministry was yanked out from underneath me. I actually ended up taking a job picking up golf balls on a golf course. I also worked at a docking station, pumping gas for commercial fishing boats.

In fact, for the next seven years I primarily worked construction jobs. And when I moved to Kansas City to join the International House of Prayer, I took a position as head of housekeeping. I cleaned the toilets! In all honesty, I felt as though God had abandoned me. The extreme reversal in my circumstances really shocked me. I went from two years of total immersion in a revival to the struggles of marriage and a series of dead-end jobs. Many times I thought about just giving up on my dreams and calling. I even questioned God's goodness.

However, in retrospect I understand that God orchestrated this seven-year "wilderness" season in order to answer the very prayers I had prayed during my time at Brownsville. When I said, "God, use me; make me holy and release Your power through my life," He took it seriously! I just didn't anticipate His methods when it came to transforming me. "Truly, truly, I say to you, unless a grain of wheat falls into the earth and dies, it remains alone; but if it dies, it bears much fruit" (John 12:24). While this period in my life was filled with death and disillusionment, it was also filled with growth.

Though I have just shared my personal experience, the broader principles are applicable to all believers. God uses the pressures of trials, dry seasons, and disappointments to sanctify and mature all of His children. Therefore, it is critical for us to recognize these patterns in our lives. God will not rescue us from the process of sanctification, even when that process is hard!

In Matthew 3 we see that Jesus had to endure the wilderness before He was released into the fullness of His calling.

> *After being baptized, Jesus came up immediately from the water; and behold, the heavens were opened, and he saw the Spirit of God descending as a dove and lighting on Him, and behold, a voice out of the heavens said, "This is My beloved Son, in whom I am well-pleased"* (Matthew 3:16-17).

I can hardly imagine a more powerful scene. A humble carpenter from Nazareth traveled to the Jordan River to be baptized by His cousin, John. When He rose from the water, the veil between worlds was temporarily lifted as heaven opened, the Holy Spirit descended in visible form, and the Father thundered His love and affirmation. The unbelievable glory of this event made what followed even more shocking:

> *Then Jesus was led up by the Spirit into the wilderness to be tempted by the devil* (Matthew 4:1).

Did you catch that? The Holy Spirit—the One who had just descended in the form of a dove as the Father proclaimed His love—led Jesus straight into a confrontation with the greatest powers of hell. This was no accident. God was after something specific in the wilderness: He wanted His Son to undergo the process of spiritual maturation and sanctification.

Let's take a closer look at that process in the life of Jesus. Two primary truths were affirmed at His baptism—who He was, and how the Father felt about Him. Who knows how much Jesus understood about His calling before this moment? His childhood and youth are hidden from us, and we are forced to use our holy imaginations to fill in the blanks. Though His baptism was probably not the first time Jesus encountered the truth concerning His identity, the word from God must have strengthened Him for the coming ordeal in the wilderness. In fact, the audible voice of affirmation was an indication of the severity of the test ahead. The greater the prophetic word, the harder the path to its fulfillment.

> The audible voice of affirmation
> was an indication of the
> severity of the test ahead.

Many of us do not stop to fully appreciate the magnitude of the test Jesus faced. We picture a man still glowing with the power of divine affirmation, triumphantly walking through the barren landscape and rebutting the devil with ease. But according to the Scriptures, Jesus was a human just like us. He suffered as we suffer. In fact, Matthew specifically mentions that after fasting forty days and nights, Jesus was hungry (see Matt. 4:2). This is probably an understatement. If you have ever fasted for any length of time, you know how overwhelming the sensations of hunger and fatigue can be. Jesus was in the middle of nowhere, with no food, no shelter, and no worship CD to encourage Him. Then, in the midst of His isolation, exhaustion, and hunger, Satan showed up.

Again, we need to remember that though He was fully God, He was also fully man. Jesus walked through this experience in His humanity, and it must have been intense! The darkness, oppression, and fear were probably earth-shaking as He stood before the ruler of hell. Have you ever been in a situation so filled with demonic activity that it made you physically sick? The first time I visited the cathedral of Notre Dame, I encountered the effects of black magic. I happened to know that a coven of witches met regularly in that place, and as soon as I crossed the threshold I could feel demonic power in the atmosphere. My back began to hurt, I felt pins and needles all over my body, I was overwhelmed by an intense headache, and I nearly passed out. This is nothing compared to what Jesus was probably feeling! At one point in their encounter, Satan even transported Jesus from one location to another. I sometimes think we miss that element when we read this story, yet it serves to illustrate just how much demonic power was present during this test.

The enemy immediately went after the prophetic declaration Jesus received at His baptism. The first words out of his mouth were, "If You are the Son of God" (Matt. 4:3). There are many reasons why Jesus chose to lean on Scripture when He responded to this onslaught of doubt and temptation, but one of those reasons was that His own strength was depleted. He accepted the weakness of His humanity and chose to rely solely on the strength of the Word of God.

The result of this confrontation was a fresh anointing:

> *When the devil had finished every temptation, he left Him until an opportune time. And Jesus returned to Galilee **in the power of the Spirit**, and news about Him spread through all the surrounding district* (Luke 4:13-14).

Whenever I read the phrase, "in the power of the Spirit," I am reminded of my early experiences at the Brownsville Revival. I have been around men and women who carried such an intense anointing of the Holy Spirit that you could feel power radiating from them even if you were standing fifteen feet away. I have also experienced what it is like to minister with this kind of anointing. I once prayed for a crowd of three thousand people in less than thirty minutes—entire rows of men and women were falling down under the power of God before I even reached them. But all this is nothing compared to the power and anointing that must have rested on Jesus when He emerged from the wilderness. I bet people could feel the presence of God that rested on Him a mile away!

> What we may think is a demonic assault could actually be the discipline of the Lord or a God-ordained test meant to establish us in our identity.

Jesus was already filled with the Holy Spirit, but now He was endued with power. The season had shifted, and it was time for Him to enter into His ministry.

> *And He came to Nazareth, where He had been brought up; and as was His custom, He entered the synagogue on the Sabbath, and stood up to read. And the book of the prophet Isaiah was handed to Him. And He opened the book and found the place where it was written,*
>
> *"The Spirit of the Lord is upon Me, because He anointed Me to preach the gospel to the poor. He*

has sent Me to proclaim release to the captives,
and recovery of sight to the blind, to set free those
who are oppressed, to proclaim the favorable year
of the Lord" (Luke 4:16-19).

His next declaration was birthed from His victory in the wilderness: "Today this Scripture has been fulfilled in your hearing" (Luke 4:21). I like to picture Jesus walking into Nazareth, power radiating from His being and fire burning in His eyes as He takes up the scroll of Isaiah and declares, "The Spirit of the Lord is upon Me." He was unshakably confident in His identity and calling, and even the demons trembled before Him (see Luke 4:33-34).

As believers, we experience this same progression of seasons. Our hearts are refined and we are prepared to receive the power and anointing of the Spirit through seasons of delay, resistance, and temptation. Knowing this will help us discern how and when to engage in spiritual warfare and deliverance. What we may think is a demonic assault could actually be the discipline of the Lord or a God-ordained test meant to establish us in our identity. First Chronicles 12:32 describes the sons of Issachar as "men who understood the times, with knowledge of what Israel should do." This verse highlights the value of studying the ways of God. When we understand the various times and seasons that comprise the journey of sanctification, it empowers us to move forward in every season and protects us from disillusionment.

After we are saved, we receive the love and affirmation of God. He tells us who we are and gives us prophetic promises related to our calling. This is a sweet time of affection and encouragement. Our hearts are captivated by the goodness of God and His plans for us. Often this season is accompanied by emotional healing and restoration. We are filled with new love, the revelation of our identity, and excitement for the future.

> We cannot always be led by our emotions. Faith is increased when we declare biblical truths despite what we feel (or don't feel).

Then the wilderness closes in around us, and the enemy mounts his attack. "Did God really say that? Can He really use someone like you? Is He even trustworthy?" Demonic spirits work to undermine our confidence in who God is and how He feels about us. Once we begin to doubt, we are presented with opportunities to circumvent the divine timing of our ministry. The enemy delights in taking advantage of our discouragement when we are in a season of waiting for the release of prophetic promises. He tempts us to move forward in our own strength and fulfill our calling prematurely, knowing this will produce offense and bitterness in our hearts and eventually cause us to reject the very assignment we received from the Father.

During my wilderness season I had to choose to believe God's promises concerning my calling, even when my circumstances seemed hopeless. This required me to battle my doubt and trust God at a deeper level than I ever had before. In the process I learned to not be so easily offended when my prayers seemed to go unanswered. And I learned to love God even when it was hard.

You see, if we resist the temptation to walk according to the flesh and pass the tests of the wilderness, we will progress in spiritual maturity. Authentic faith will develop in our lives, and we will receive increased anointing and power. This is an important point: when we do not feel God's presence we have the opportunity to strengthen our dependence on the Word of God. We cannot always be led by our emotions. Faith is increased when we declare biblical truths despite what we feel (or don't feel). Many believers are tempted to just give up when God's tangible presence lifts, but if we press in and continue to believe His promises, we will receive even more from Him when the season of manifestation comes. At the end of the day, God is more concerned with our maturity than our happiness, and He is more interested in developing our character than our comfort. As the psalmist says, "Blessed be the Lord, my rock, who trains my hands for war, and my fingers for battle" (Ps. 144:1). Though the journey is sometimes hard, we can rest in the assurance that God is at work in our lives, producing greater holiness and preparing us for greater victories over darkness.

In Luke 4:13, it says the devil left Jesus "until an opportune time." Though Satan was unsuccessful in his first open confrontation with Jesus, he was determined to renew his attack when the opportunity arose. During the course of His ministry Jesus was assaulted by a mob (see Luke 4:28-30), questioned by Pharisees who sought to trap Him in His words (see Matt. 22:15-18), betrayed by His own disciple, and sentenced by the Roman authorities. In other words, the enemy doesn't easily retreat or concede defeat. We will all experience multiple seasons of warfare and testing throughout the course of our lives. This is why Paul instructs the believers in Ephesus to "stand firm" three separate times when he writes to them concerning spiritual warfare (see Eph. 6:10-17).

FROM GLORY TO GLORY

In my life, the desire for more of God has set me on a collision course with the enemy—and I am sure there are many believers who would say the same. When we get serious about our pursuit of the kingdom, we can become a magnet for spiritual warfare. This is why it is so important to educate the Body of Christ concerning deliverance ministry and corporate intercession. It is equally important, however, to remember that our primary goal is not defeating the enemy but rather receiving more from God. This is a subtle yet necessary shift in focus. It is very easy to become distracted by the all-too-real dynamics of warfare and end up disconnected from the heart of God.

One of the greatest examples of a man who refused to be overwhelmed or sidetracked by the enemy is Moses. First of all, the warfare he encountered makes most of our struggles look small by comparison. He confronted the superpower of his day, faced off against the most elite practitioners of black magic, and participated in the defeat of an entire army. And then there are the signs and wonders he experienced—the ten plagues, the parting of the Red Sea, miraculous food and water appearing in the middle of the desert, not to mention the giant pillar of cloud and fire that led the way to Mount Sinai. When he arrived at the mountain, Moses and seventy elders climbed into the thick darkness and shared a meal with God.

After all these events, however, Moses had one request—he wanted to see God's glory. Stop for a moment and think about this request. Wouldn't you say that he already had seen the glory of God? What more could there possibly be to see? Yet God replied that Moses could only look at His back. In fact, He actually covered Moses with His hand until after He had passed by him on the mountain. In that moment Moses received one of the most profound revelations of God's heart in the history of humanity. He was allowed to draw closer than ever before as God revealed Himself in a strikingly vulnerable proclamation: "The Lord, the Lord God, compassionate and gracious, slow to anger, and abounding in lovingkindness and truth; who keeps lovingkindness for thousands, who forgives iniquity, transgression and sin" (Exod. 34:6-7).

Moses was not sidetracked by the intense warfare surrounding Israel's departure from Egypt, and he was not lulled into complacency by the many signs and wonders he had already witnessed. No, Moses had discovered that the glory of God is *infinite*, and he was determined that nothing less than the ever-increasing revelation of that glory would satisfy him. He was consumed by the desire for God's presence.

When I consider the life of Moses, I am filled with fresh hope. As a young believer I used to be incredibly discouraged by the thought of eternity. I pictured myself sitting on a cloud with a harp, singing songs to God and dying of boredom. But the story of Moses changed this picture for me. After all of the astounding miracles he witnessed, Moses still wanted more. He had an insatiable appetite for God, and I realized that this exciting hunger was available to me as well.

There is so much more for us to see and experience in God. There is a never-ending fountain of fascination springing up from within the Trinity, and we can drink as deeply as we like. The battle against darkness is not eternal. There is coming a day when Satan and his demons will be forever condemned to hell and all warfare will finally cease. But the revelation of God is infinite. We will spend eternity discovering the wonders of His nature, His character, and His heart. Let us seek to live our lives in light of this reality. Let us declare along with Moses that our deepest desire is to see the glory of God.

ABOUT
STEPHEN BEAUCHAMP

STEPHEN BEAUCHAMP IS THE DIRECTOR OF PROPHETIC, Healing, and Deliverance training at International House of Prayer University in Kansas City, Missouri and has been in the deliverance ministry for over ten years. Stephen and his wife, Sage, are both graduates of the Brownsville Revival School of Ministry and are itinerate all over the world spreading the message of spiritual revival.

For inquiries about speaking engagements, please contact Stephen at: stephenbeauchamp@ihopkc.org.